For Maggie and Fritz—

With much love and
all good wishes.

August 1973

The Secret Jews

The Secret Jews

JOACHIM PRINZ

 RANDOM HOUSE NEW YORK

LIBRARY OF CONGRESS CATALOGING IN PUBLICATION DATA
Prinz, Joachim, 1902–
The secret Jews.
Bibliography: p.
1. Maranos. 2. Sephardim. I. Title.
DS124.P74 910'.039'24 73-5024
ISBN 0-394-47204-7

For my grandchildren
Adam, Barak, Jesse, Jim,
Nancy, Tammy and Tom

"It is of no use to Your Majesty to pour Holy water on the Jews and call them Peter or Paul, while they adhere to their religion like Akiba or Tarphon. There is no advantage in their baptism except to make them overweening against true Christians and without fear, since outwardly they are accepted as Christians. The royal tribute which they used to pay when they were Jews they pay no more. Know, Sire, that Judaism is no doubt one of the incurable diseases."

—Solomon Ibn Verga
Spain, fifteenth century

I wish to thank my daughter, Lucie Prinz, for the valuable work she did to bring this book to its present form. It was a labor of love and of great skill for which I am very grateful.

The Secret Jews

Chapter One

In a remote Brazilian village, on the wall of an old hut, a visitor in recent years found a parchment covered with strange symbols. It was hanging among the traditional holy pictures with which a pious Catholic decorates his home. The owner of the hut knew nothing about the parchment except that it had been a cherished family possession for many centuries.

In another hut the visitor found a woman who remembered a strange custom observed by her father. Once a year, in the fall, he would wrap himself in a white sheet with black stripes and pray from a special book—which had unfortunately been lost. "On that day," she said, "my father would not eat from one night to the next." Moreover, there was one custom which every household in that village observed. On Friday night a white tablecloth was spread in each hut and candles were lit. Nobody knew why. "It has always been that way with us," they said.

Some members of the upper classes of Brazil also observe this weekly ritual. The wealthy women of Rio de Janeiro lead a sheltered monotonous life. A combination of rigid

Spanish and Catholic custom restricts them to church, family and social activities. So, for many of them, the routine revolves around a daily card game which occupies them for most of the afternoon. But on Fridays, in certain communities, the cards are put away earlier than usual so that the ladies can get home before sunset to spread a white cloth on the table and light the candles. When asked by a Brazilian scholar why they did this, some said, "In honor of the Prince of Peace." But not much solemnity is attached to this ceremony. No prayers are said. It is as though they were merely arranging flowers in a vase. Most of these devout Catholic women would be amazed if they were told that they were welcoming the Sabbath in accordance with ancient Jewish tradition.

In fact, the old woman who has marked the eastern wall of her hut with an ancient parchment called *mizrah* (usually hung in an Orthodox Jewish home to indicate the direction the man of the house should face when saying his prayers); the man who wraps himself in a prayer shawl and fasts once a year during the season, and perhaps on the very day, when Jews fast to observe the Day of Atonement; and the Brazilian women, rich and poor, who light candles and set a festive table on Friday nights are all, whether they are aware of it or not, demonstrating their ties to the faith of a common ancestor. They are descendants of the Marranos, those Spanish Jews who converted to Catholicism but who remained, secretly, practicing Jews and who handed their tradition down from one generation to the next.

Today in many parts of the world, there are people who now practice various religions but who have retained vestiges of their Jewish heritage in their customs or rituals. For some, like the ladies of Rio de Janeiro, what was once the family's pious act has become a social amenity. Others are more conscious of their Marrano past and may include some Jewish words or customs in their worship services. Some have even returned to the original faith of their ancestors.

Once, in 1950, when I delivered a lecture in Santiago, Chile, I was asked to receive a delegation of apparently good, faithful Christians who were collecting money for the purchase of land in Israel through the Jewish National Fund. They confessed that this was their link to their Jewish past. When I asked how they knew about their heritage they said, "Our fathers passed it down to us, as they received this knowledge from their parents and grandparents. We recognized each other because each of us observed the Sabbath, fasted on the Day of Atonement and kept other Jewish customs." Today this group of Marranos call themselves Sons of Zion and have emigrated to Argentina, where they live in a commune in preparation for their emigration to Israel. They celebrate their own version of the Passover meal, the Seder. It is held in a Marranic synagogue in Buenos Aires and it lasts all night. The women wear white dresses and black veils. They greet each other with a kiss on the forehead. This is the way those of their forefathers who were convicted by the tribunal of the Inquisition greeted each other in the fifteenth century.

Although Marranos, covert Jews, have come to be linked in the minds of most people with the Spain of the Inquisition (and most present-day Marranos *are* decendants of Spanish Jews), Jewish existence in disguise predates the Inquisition by more than a thousand years. The Visigoths promulgated the first anti-Jewish laws when they ruled Spain. The first anti-Jewish riots in Spain took place in the fourth century, when Christianity was in its fledgling years. It was then that Jews were first coerced into embracing Christianity, but many of them did so while continuing to cling to Jewish customs and beliefs. Little is known about the early Spanish Marranos. They were few in number and finally merged with the rest of the population. There were also cases of Marranos in the Byzantine Empire, and even in Africa (although all traces of them have vanished).

Nor is Marranism restricted to Christian lands. In the nineteenth century, during a period of national and religious unrest in Persia, several Jewish communities were annihilated. Many of the survivors became Mohammedans but continued to practice their Jewish customs. Their descendants live in a ghetto in the holy city of Meshed in present-day Iran. They were originally called Djedid al Islam, converts to Islam. Today they are permitted to practice Judaism in addition to Islam, and they have Hebraized their Arabic names. They call themselves *jadidim* and they exhibit what is probably the most curious form of contemporary Marranism.

On the surface they are practicing Mohammedans. They participate fully in the great pilgrimages to the holy places in the city. They can be seen mingling with other Mohammedans in the mosque but everyone knows that they constitute a community of their own, a unique Mohammedan sect with their own additional religion and with Hebrew as the language of their prayers.

They pray five times a day, as the Koran commands: ". . . wherefore glorify God, when the evening overtaketh you and when ye rise in the morning and unto him be praised in heaven and earth and in the evening and when ye rest at noon." The Mohammedan text varies only slightly from the injunction to the Jew who must pray: ". . . when thou liest down and when thou risest up." The Jews pray only three times a day; the *jadidim* evidently do not mind adding two more prayers.

They fast during the holy weeks of Ramadan and also on Yom Kippur, the Jewish Day of Atonement. They celebrate all the Jewish as well as the Mohammedan holidays, but economic necessity forces them to keep their shops open on the Jewish Sabbath. So they have developed a unique way of doing business without violating the Sabbath commandment. They put a young boy, not yet thirteen, not yet a bar mitzvah, and therefore exempt from observing the Jewish law, in charge of the shop. If one asks for the proprietor the boy will answer, as if by rote: "This is the Sabbath. My father is sick. He is always sick on the Sabbath."

Almost a hundred years after their incomplete conversion the *jadidim* retain a dual allegiance to the law of the Koran and that of the Torah which poses neither a religious nor a psychological problem for them. They bury their dead in the Mohammedan cemetery, but they wash the body in accordance with Jewish customs, say prayers for the dead and observe the prescribed seven days of mourning. Their weddings are performed by the Mohammedan cadi, but as soon as the ceremony is over they return to the home of the bridegroom's parents and recite the ancient Hebrew blessings. Since the Mohammedans, like the Jews, abstain from eating pork, the *jadidim* have only a few dietary restrictions to add; and although the rabbinic prohibition against mixing meat with milk is now forgotten, the rudiments of the Jewish dietary laws are among the many Jewish customs still observed by these strange, only partly hidden Jews.

Another group of Mohammedan Jews are the *daggatus*,

the Jewish Bedouin of the Sahara. Few people know of these secret Jews. We don't know how many of them still roam the desert since there is no census in the Sahara. Their base, if their home grounds can be called that, is in the little town of Beja. In the 1920s one of their many visitors, Nahum Slouschz, a French Jewish scholar, wrote:

The Jews of the Sahara Desert are highway robbers like those among whom they live. Even when they pray, they carry a rifle. They know nothing of the Talmud, or for that matter, of monogamy. Elohim [one of the Jewish names of God] is already forgotten and the Beth Hamidrash [the Jewish school] they know little about. They have some notion that there is a tradition according to which the Messiah will come on Tisha B'av and he will be riding on a horse wearing a white robe. The Bedouin Jews ride through the night of Tisha B'av wearing their best garments, looking at every caravan to discover whether the Messiah has arrived. When they saw me, a bearded man whom they did not know, riding with a Jewish guide, they were certain that I was the Redeemer. And it took me a long time to convince them that I was not the Messiah, but simply a professor from Paris.

In a sense the *daggatus*, like the *jadidim*, are now only playing at being Marranos. They no longer need to practice their Jewish customs clandestinely. The *jadidim* could worship in an ordinary synagogue, but they prefer to pray in underground sanctuaries, still posting women at the doors during the services to warn of approaching danger. It is no longer a necessity, only a reminder of a time when they were forced to worship in secret. It is a strange twist that the *jadidim* and the *daggatus* cling to their Marranism in the same way their forefathers did in Spain, although they are now in fact really free to be full-fledged Jews. So powerful is the effect of "religion in hiding" that it imprints the forced practices of persecution onto the lives of the people even into future generations.

There have, of course, been other examples throughout history of people who have been persecuted for their religious beliefs and who chose to worship secretly. Perhaps the best-known are the early Christians who hid in the catacombs of Rome, forbidden to say their prayers until Constantine the Great elevated their secret sect to the status of the official Church of Rome. There have been many pious deviates, persecuted by the established church or government, who left their homeland to found new religions or worship their old faiths freely. But nowhere is there any real parallel to the story of the secret Jews, the Marranos. These hidden Jews, whose strange customs have survived into our own day, are a phenomenon as singular as the Jews themselves. They are, in a sense, a vivid illustration of the mysterious, indefinable essence of Jewish history. They can be said to constitute a prototype of the uniqueness of Jewish existence. For if the Marranos are a fascinating enigma, the Jews are part of the same puzzle.

The question is really not the so-often-asked "What is a Jew?" but "Why are the Jews still around? Why have they so stubbornly survived so many centuries of persecution, dispersal and disaster?" Some have tried to explain this by referring to the Jews' claim that they are "the Chosen People." If they are chosen, it would seem that they have more often been elected for misery and exclusion, ghettos or death, than for a comfortable, peaceful or specially favored existence. Others have called the existential quality of the Jews the "Jewish mystique." But it is more of a mystery than a mystique. And the existence of Marranos, who have continued to remember their Jewish heritage and allegiance for centuries after their forefathers converted, provides a very particular and illuminating aspect of this puzzle and of the singularity of the Jewish phenomenon.

What has caused Marranism to survive? Why is there no equally persistent example in other religions? Isn't their continued existence, however tenuous their Jewish bonds, however faint their Jewish memories, part of that strange circumstance—the Jew in our midst?

The Jews are survivors of a civilization and faith born four thousand years ago. Although there are older civilizations which still flourish today, they developed in their own lands, self-contained and naturally self-perpetuating. It is also true that many of the ancient people who played an important role in antiquity still exist. But while some of the temples of Zeus and Apollo still stand, their ancient deities no longer play a part in contemporary Greek life. But the Jews, who survived in their enemies' territories, who were exiled from their own countries and then often forced to flee from the countries of their exile, still worship the God of their ancestors. They recite psalms and say prayers almost three thousand years old, and they still use the language in which they were written. Against all the laws of history, the Jews have survived with much of their ancient culture intact. Nor does the mystery vanish if we try to understand it in historical terms. The fact of Jewish survival remains a puzzle whether or not we can describe events or append a date or place to them.

In our recent past the establishment of the State of Israel, and the continued existence of large Jewish communities in the United States and other countries after the death of six million Jews during the Hitler regime, are but two examples of this incredible resilience. The contemporary events are not unrelated to an understanding of the Jews who more than four hundred years ago, in the face of the most dire circumstances, invented Marranism in its classical form out of a desire to remain part of the people and the faith of Israel.

We do not know how many Jews became Marranos, of a sort, under the Hitler regime. There must have been thousands who resorted to all kinds of tricks to hide their Jewishness. They forged passports and identity cards; they changed their names, dyed their hair and pretended to be Aryans. Some fled into monasteries, others were hidden in the homes of good Christians. After Hitler's defeat most of them returned to Judaism. They had never been committed to the Saviour they, for survival's sake, had pretended to worship so fervently.

A different species of hidden Jew emerged during the early days of Hitler. Families which had been living as Christians for generations suddenly came forward to return to their people. They had attended church diligently, mixed freely with their Gentile neighbors, and were accepted as equals. In fact, they considered themselves full-fledged Christians. Often their children were not told of their Jewish descent. It did not seem important.

Hitler's racial laws put an end to all this. Such people were now considered Jews in spite of their conversion and their proven devotion to Christianity. Some wavered between allegiance to their Christian faith and their sense of pride and, perhaps, a growing identification with their fellow Jews. Many of them returned to Judaism only after they had been declared Jewish by the Gestapo; many of them died as Jews in the concentration camps. But others became enthusiastic believing members of the Jewish faith, emigrating to Palestine and other countries where they could openly return to the religion of their forefathers. During the early years of the Hitler regime, I was invited to visit the head of an old banking firm which had been founded during the first decade of the nineteenth century by the sons of the Jewish philosopher Moses Mendelssohn. (One of these men was the father of Felix Mendelssohn-Bartholdy, the composer, who was baptized at birth.) When Hitler came to power the head of the banking house, Franz von Mendelssohn, a great-grandson of Christians, was president of the Lutheran Churches of Germany. He received me in his private office in an eighteenth-century château and announced that he had resigned from his office in the Church, although, even according to the anti-Jewish Nuremberg Laws, he was considered an Aryan. "I feel," he said with great emotion, "that a descendant of the Jewish philosopher Moses Mendelssohn could no longer pretend." With this, he took me to a small museum housed in is mansion. The walls were covered with many of the eighteenth-century portraits of his Jewish ancestor. A bust of the philosopher stood in the center of the room. In a glass case were the famous white porcelain monkeys which every Jew had been forced to buy at exorbitant prices in the middle of the eighteenth century to finance the Prussian porcelain industry then being established by Frederick the Great.

When we returned to his office we were both too moved to speak. Finally I said to him, "You are a Marrano." Mr. Mendelssohn had never heard the term. I then told him the story of the Marranos, and particularly of those who had returned to Judaism. "Too late," he said, "too late for me. I and my ancestors have been brought up as believing Christians for four generations. I can only return to my people, not to its faith. I identify myself with their pain, their fate, their pride." He did not return to Judaism, but his daughter, Eleanora von Mendelssohn, a well-known actress, became an Orthodox Jew.

In Hitler's Germany, as so often before in Jewish history, persecution stimulated Jewish resilience and inspired a return to Jewish values. Oppression has repeatedly awakened the Jews' dormant resources and created contempt for the persecutor; the result has often been a renascence of Judaism. This is not to deny that many Jews did convert under the pressure of the Inquisition and the terror of the Gestapo. There were certainly many thousands of sincere converts who became devout Christians and totally gave up their Judaism. But the phenomenon, which may contain at least a partial answer to the riddle of the survival of the Jewish people, is that through centuries of persecution in each generation there have always been Jews who maintain their Jewishness in some way, and that to the present time their descendants manifest the memory of their ancestors' faith in their rituals and their lives.

A more complicated aspect of this phenomenon occurred recently in Russia. At the turn of the century young Russian Jews, whose forefathers had suffered for decades under the czar's savage pogroms, were among the early converts to Communism and followed the lead of Marx, Trotsky and the other early Communist theoreticians—who themselves were Jews, though, of course, not observant Jews. To rid themselves of every vestige of their Jewish heritage and to demonstrate their allegiance to the new system, which scorned religion of any kind, some staged wild parties on the Day of Atonement, while the remnant of the faithful Jews were saying their prayers. (For those who wanted to retain their Jewish identity, early Communism provided a measure of religious freedom; some schools still taught Yiddish, many synagogues remained open.) The young Jewish students, marching under the red banner with their fellow Russians, were ecstatic about their sudden and glorious emancipation from the Pale of Settlement, those areas of the country to which Jews had been confined since the end of the nineteenth century. They became super-Communists, freed from the daily degradation, the insults and the recurrent pogroms which had become part of the history of the Russian Jews under the czars. The new political dogma seemed to promise that this sort of persecution would never occur again.

The anti-Semitic brutality of the Stalin regime showed this Jewish euphoria to have been a fool's paradise. The Jewish schools were closed; most of the synagogues were boarded up. Hundreds of Jewish intellectuals and professionals, all fervent Communists, were exterminated in the purges. Soviet Jewry's Marranic period had begun. But it remained a rather quiet, even dormant form of secret Judaism until the creation of the State of Israel.

The Russian Jews, who had lived isolated so long from the world Jewish community, suddenly had an Israeli embassy in Moscow. They heard Hebrew spoken, listened to the Voice of Israel on their radios, saw the Star of David, which they had learned to hide, publicly displayed on the flag of the new state. Young Russian Jews who had never read a Jewish book suddenly rediscovered their Judaism. In their case it took the form not of a return to the religious precepts of their forefathers, but of a new nationalism focused on the State of Israel.

The ultimate stimulus, however, came from the Six-Day War, in 1967. What had lain dormant in the minds of thousands of Russian Jews now involved hundreds of thousands, young and old. In 1967 young Communists—still, of course, unwilling to pray in the temple, but no longer mocking the observant Jews who chose to—celebrated the gay festival of the giving of the law, Simchat Torah, by dancing the Horah and singing Hebrew songs in Moscow's Synagogue Square.

During the twenty-five years since the creation of the State of Israel, thousands of Russian Jews have met secretly to learn Hebrew as did the Marranos in Spain and Portugal. Outwardly faithful Communists who go to party meetings, they live a clandestine Jewish life, preparing themselves for emigration to Israel. They still make up a tiny minority of the three and a half million Soviet Jews, but the Marranos are a significant fact of Jewish life in Russia. They would like to leave their double lives of deceit and make-believe. During the past ten years many thousands have gone to live in Israel.

Though this book will concentrate on other periods of history and on other peoples, the covert Jews of the Soviet Union are no less Marranos than were the fifteenth-century Jews of the Iberian Peninsula.

Chapter Two

In 1971 I was visiting a Canadian Jewish scholar who
showed me his collection of Jewish ceremonial objects.
Wine cups, precious velvet coverings for the holy scrolls,
and many other rare and beautiful things used for Jewish
ceremonies were displayed in his home. On a table, in what
was obviously a place of honor, stood a highly ornamented
vase. I found it clumsy and graceless and could not understand why it had been singled out for such prominence.
The more I looked at it, the less I liked it. But then my host
took the vase deftly in his hands and twisted it a bit. It
opened easily, and to my amazement, proved not to be a
vase at all. It was a veritable treasure house of every ritual
object used in a Jewish home, each of them in miniature:
a goblet for the holy-day wine, a tiny eight-branched
candlestick for the celebration of Hanukkah—the feast of
lights—a spice box for the ceremony at the end of the
Sabbath, and many others.

"I bought it in Spain," my friend said. "This is a replica
of a vase found in the home of a Spanish Marrano. On
ordinary days it stood in the living room, filled with flowers.

When the Sabbath or a Jewish holiday came, it provided everything the family needed to celebrate in accordance with the tradition of their Jewish ancestors." Here was an elaborate, ingenious example of the lengths to which the hidden Jews of Spain had to go to preserve their Jewishness.

To understand the nature of these furtive worshipers, the crypto-Jews of Spain, we must first explore the historic context in which this unparalleled phenomenon arose. And an examination of the strange name by which they were called may, in itself, be illuminating.

The origins of the word "Marrano" are obscure. Originally those who became Catholics in Spain, whether Jew or Moslem, were known simply as *conversos*, those who converted. But when the number of converted Jews swelled to more than ten thousand in the fourteenth century, they began to form a visible part of the Spanish population, and the distinction between the New Christians, *cristianos nuevos*, and the original Old Christians became one of the major political issues. "I am an old Christian," says Sancho Panza in *Don Quixote*. "And to become an Earl that is sufficient."

The word *marrano* undoubtedly was coined by the people and is a term of contempt and derision. Some scholars believe that it comes from the Spanish word *marrar*, meaning to deviate from truth or justice, a description of the Jews who *marran*, or mar, the true faith with insincere conversion. There are others who think it is derived from a Spanish word meaning something like prostitute. But most people agree that Marrano simply means "swine" and expresses in the simplest terms the hatred of the populace for the *cristianos nuevos*, the new—but not real—Christians. The modern Spanish dictionary lists *marrano* as "pig, hog, dirty man, cursed, excommunicated, and Jew."

But the history of the Jew in Spain predates not only the word but the contempt that it clearly expresses. No Jewish community in the world—outside of Palestine—was older than that of the Iberian Peninsula. Long before Spain existed as a political entity, Jews lived there. When the prophet Jonah undertook his foolish flight from God in the fourth century B.C., he boarded "a ship that was going to Tarshish." Nor did he take just any boat. The Bible says that "Jonah rose up to flee to Tarshish." The ancient Tarshish has been identified as the Spanish harbor town of Cádiz, at the estuary of the river Guadalquivir in Andalusia. Jonah would hardly have planned to travel to Tarshish, so far from home, had he not known that he would find people there who spoke his language and worshiped the God of Israel.

It is due to the antiquity of the Spanish Jewish community that the Sephardim, as the Spanish Jews are called, considered themselves the aristocracy of the Jewish people. The Jew's long history in Spain is probably the reason for his affluence, his creativity and his impact on the country. It may also account for his identification with Spain, his almost total acculturation and, subsequently, his weakness.

Unlike the Jew of Eastern Europe, who spoke Yiddish in his ghetto, the Spanish Jew spoke Arabic under Arab rule and every Spanish dialect when he lived under the rule and protection of the Christian kings. While the Jews in Spain always lived in their own quarters, these *juderías* more closely resembled the American Jewish neighborhood than the degrading walled ghetto of medieval Europe or the Pale of Settlement in which Jews were forced to live under the czars. The houses of the Spanish Jews were frequently large and comfortable, and they were usually in close proximity to the castle or the bishopric of their protector. Often when the areas became too small for a growing Jewish population, new *judería* streets were added. And although some *juderías* had gates, for centuries no walls were needed to protect them from attack or to confine them to their neighborhoods.

There are no exact statistics about the number of Jews who lived in Spain, but the total population of the country was approximately eleven million at the end of the Christian Reconquest in the fourteenth century. The Jewish population, always listed as "household" (that is, families which paid special taxes to the crown or to the bishop), was small. It is reasonable to assume that the Jewish community never amounted to more than half a million people.

Under a rule established by the Visigoths, the Jews were not permitted to own land. But as the chronicler Andrés Bernáldez has recorded, they were prominent in all other fields. Bernáldez tells us that they were "merchants, salesmen, taxgatherers, retailers, stewards of the nobility, officials, tailors, shoemakers, tanners, weavers, grocers, peddlers, silk merchants, smiths, jewellers, and other like trades." This list makes it clear that they were firmly established in the lower-middle class of the country. But it omits the amazing involvement of the Jews in government, high finance and the sciences.

During the reign of the Moors, with but few interruptions, the Spanish Jews enjoyed not merely an equality of rights not accorded Jews in other European countries until the French Revolution; they held positions of great honor and distinction. There was hardly a Cabinet during the period between the eighth century and the Christian Reconquest which did not have a Jew serving as minister of finance. And the importance of the Jews in government did not diminish under the rule of the Christian kings. The historian Valeriu Marcu has described their role:

These Jews, who were for the most part rich, consciously furthered the great process of national construction. Through its exalted representatives Jewish wealth fulfilled a political function quite outside Jewry. In the domain of culture the part played by the Jews was not less significant. The contact between the Christian and Arabian worlds, which was so important for Western Europe, took place through the intermediary of the Jews. The expelled Arabs had bequeathed to them the inheritance of Hellenism, and the brilliant universities of the Caliphs at Cordoba and Toledo continued their activities under Christian rule—and the guidance of the Jews. Jewish scholars had once competed with the Moors in translating into Arabic the works of Plato, Aristotle, Ptolemy and the Greek mathematicians and scientists, and they now translated these further into Castilian. Not only were they translators, but they were among the first to produce original literature in the Castilian tongue; they stood at the cradle of Spanish and they moulded it from a dialect into a language.

Everything that the Jews had achieved in the fields of chemistry, astrology, mathematics and medicine in their collaboration with the Arabs they now handed on alone. They were enthusiastic proclaimers of experimental science and science was practically their monopoly. Throughout the whole of Spain the art of medicine was in their hands. The personal physicians of the grandees, the kings and the archbishops were all Jews. Even the pious rabbis, who had once opposed the cultural alliance of Jews and Arabs and still proscribed the scientific work of the Jews, made an exception in the case of medicine.

While thousands of Jews suffered in the rest of Europe, while the crusaders murdered them in the Rhineland and wherever they carried the cross toward Palestine in their holy war, Spanish Jewry celebrated its Golden Era. But it turned out to be only a prolonged interlude. By the fourteenth century the peace of the Spanish Jew was also nearing its end. In the wake of the Crusades, all of Europe had been engulfed in Jew-baiting masquerading as Christian piety. There was hardly a country where the Jew could live in safety, and in Spain, too, the stage was being set for the end of the peaceful existence of the Jews, although their traditional positions of power continued to protect them for some time. Later, in Spain's attempt to make the entire country Christian, synagogues as well as mosques were often burned. The Lateran Councils of 1179 and 1215 promulgated an anti-Jewish policy which was embodied, in Spain in 1256, in the Seven Part Code of Alfonso the Wise. While the code was not enforced until much later, Jews were often victims of local civil battles. Although at the court of the king they enjoyed many privileges, they were subjected to the anti-Jewish statutes of the towns in which they lived. Valeriu Marcu points out this irony:

The impetus of those who directed the force of their hostility against the Jews was stronger than the most well-meaning royal will. The walls of the ghettos did not, of course, impinge on the royal palaces, and daily contact was only with hate-filled subjects. Like the ghettos, the towns possessed their autonomy, their fueros or statutes, and the Christian fueros were arrayed against the Jewish ones. They wanted to enclose the Jews in their Jewries. The king might do with his Jews what he would, but the towns desired to keep them out of their territory. It could therefore come to pass that Jews, to whom every state office was open and who determined the policy of the country as semi-dictators, were not allowed to use the same bath-houses as the Christians or appear as witnesses before Christian tribunals. In strict contrast to the royal patents, the town tried to deprive the Jews of the right to carry on a trade or enter into commercial transactions outside the ghetto and defamed them wherever possible.

In 1348, when King Henry II came to power, Alfonso's Seven Part Code and its anti-Jewish restrictions became the law of the land. The code restricted everyday existence, although it very clearly guaranteed that Jewish lives be spared:

Jews are a people, who, although they do not believe in the religion of Our Lord Jesus Christ, yet, the great Christian sovereigns have always permitted them to live among . . .

. . . The reason that the church emperors, kings and princes permitted the Jews to dwell among them, and with Christians, is because they always lived, as it were, in captivity, as it was constantly a token in the minds of men that they were descended from those who crucified Our Lord Jesus Christ.

The code prohibited the Jews from building new synagogues except in places where they had been torn down. The new buildings could not be "made larger or raised to any greater height" than the old ones they replaced. Nor could they be made luxurious or painted. But the code also protected the houses of worship:

For the reason that a synagogue is a place where the name of God is praised we forbid any Christian to deface it, or remove anything from it, or take anything out of it by force . . . Moreover we forbid Christians to put any animal into a synagogue, or loiter in it or place any hindrance in the way of the Jews while they are there performing their devotions according to their religion.

Respect and even reverence for the faith and the customs of the Jew were meticulously decreed by the code. Inferior though Judaism was, "the name of God" which is "praised in the synagogue" must be duly honored. There is a particularly touching paragraph about the Sabbath:

Sabbath is the day on which Jews perform their devotions, and remain quiet in their lodgings, and do not make contracts or transact any business; and for the reason that they are obliged by their religion to keep it, no one should on that day summon them or bring them into court. Therefore we order that no judge shall employ force or any constraint upon Jews on Saturdays in order to bring them into court on account of their debts; or arrest them; or cause them any other annoyance. . . .

The most startling part of the Seven Part Code dealt with the problem of Jews who converted to Christianity. Remember that these high-sounding thoughts were written only a few decades before thousands of Jews were coerced to convert. A few years later the new converts were being treated with contempt by the community, and finally tortured and killed by the Inquisition. But the Seven Part Code stated that

No force or compulsion shall be employed in any way against a Jew to induce him to become a Christian; but Christians should convert him to the faith of Our Lord Jesus Christ by means of the texts of the Holy Scriptures and by kind words, for no one can love or appreciate a service which is done him by compulsion. We also decree that if any Jew or Jewess should voluntarily desire to become a Christian, the other Jews shall not interfere with this in any way. . . . and we also order that, after any Jews become Christians, all persons in our dominions shall honor them; and that no one shall dare to reproach them or their descendants, by way of insult, with having been Jews; and that they shall possess all their property, sharing the same with their brothers and inheriting it from their fathers and mothers and other relatives, just as if they were Jews; and that they can hold all offices and dignities which other Christians can do.

All these pronouncements were but a pious preamble to the most brutal anti-Jewish restrictions. While the Seven Part Code decreed benevolence toward the Jewish faith, the attitude toward the people was specific and harsh:

We forbid any Jew to keep Christian men or women in his house, to be served by them; although he may have them to cultivate and take care of his lands, or protect him on the way when he is compelled to go to some dangerous place. Moreover, we forbid any Christian man or woman to invite a Jew or a Jewess, or to accept an invitation from them, to eat or drink together or to drink any wine made by their hands. We also order that no Jews shall dare to bathe in company with Christians, and that no Christian shall take any medicine or cathartic made by a Jew. . . .

Jews who dared to live with Christians were put to death. Sexual relations between Jews and Christian women "who are spiritually the wives of Our Lord Jesus Christ because of the faith and baptism which they receive in His name" deserved capital punishment. Even a Christian prostitute could not degrade herself by having "carnal intercourse with either Moor or Jew." Furthermore, Jews were suspected of celebrating Good Friday contemptuously, "stealing children and fastening them to crosses or making images of wax and crucifying them when they cannot obtain children."

Far from being a theological, doctrinal declaration of the Church, the Seven Part Code was in reality a prelude, if not an invitation, to mass murder. The ancient battle of the Church for domination over secular powers had been won a hundred years before the anti-Jewish laws of Spain were promulgated. No king, no duke, no municipal government was free. Their dependence upon the clergy, both local and papal, was a fact of medieval life.

As in other countries, the church laws, often translated into the laws of the states, were only a pious reflection of the people's reaction to the Jews whose foreign customs and whose denial and rejection of the divinity of Christ infuriated the devout. Envy and jealousy of Jewish commercial ingenuity and success fanned the flames of hatred among the masses.

Anti-Jewish feelings grew during the years following the enactment of the Seven Part Code. King Juan of Castile succeeded Henry II, and when he died in 1390, his infant son assumed the throne. The queen who ruled during her son's minority was greatly influenced by her confessor, Ferrand Martínez, administrator of the archdiocese of Seville and a sworn enemy of the Jews. In 1391, from his pulpit in the great cathedral of Seville, Martínez called for the destruction of the twenty-three synagogues in the city. Whether the Church stimulated the bloodshed or whether it only yielded to popular demand, we do not know. In any case, on June 4, 1391, the Jewish community of Seville was destroyed by a mob that stormed the Jewish sectors and burned the synagogues. It was the beginning of a storm which swept the whole country.

Whatever caused anti-Jewish riots in other countries, the Spanish massacres can only be understood as a part of the effort to root out all non-Catholic elements in the country and unite it under Catholic rule. The reconquest on which Spain embarked can be called Spain's own crusade. Spain was the holy land. While other nations marched against the infidels in Palestine, the Spanish crusaders found them right in their own country: in the Jews and the Moors. In Spanish eyes these two non-Christian peoples formed an unholy alliance. After all, the social, economic and scientific successes of the Jews were the result of hundreds of years of tolerant Arab rule. In no other country had they achieved such prominence. Nowhere else did they wield such power.

While the fervor of the European crusaders may have set the tone for the Spanish reconquest, here it was not a select group of brave men, knights and their followers who fought for the purification of the faith. In Spain a whole nation rose up in holy indignation to expatriate the evil in their body politic, to weed out the infidel, and by so doing, cleanse the land and the Church. To them it was the great battle for Christ, in the course of which they would not only succeed in making Spain a country free of non-Christians but also rid themselves of the most formidable economic competitors in their daily lives, the Jews.

The riots which had begun in Seville spread to Córdoba. On June 20, 1391, the Jews of Toledo were massacred. Only two of the city's many synagogues were left standing. The pogrom was blamed by the municipal authorities on the *pueblo menudo,* the little people, the lower class. There were some official attempts to prevent the riots, but they proved unsuccessful. Not even in Segovia, the seat of the government, could the Jews be saved. Burgos was battered by the "rage of the mob." Hardly a Jewish community in Castile escaped. Aragon soon followed, in spite of official protestations, and the Jews of Valencia barricaded themselves behind the gates of the ghetto. And while authorities seemed more determined here than elsewhere to stop the mob, nothing helped. One of the rioters was hanged in front of the ghetto, but in spite of this gruesome warning the frenzied mob smashed the gates and two hundred and fifty Jews were killed. And so it went in brutal monotony from one town to the other. The gang leaders who stormed into the Jewish quarters and killed the Jews in their synagogues carried the crucifix together with the sword. To them the Jews were "traitors, homosexuals, child murderers, blasphemers, assassins, poisoners and usurpers." Because they were accused of having killed Christ, they were now to be killed in his name.

The merciless violence soon moved swiftly from the mainland to the Balearic Islands, which had a large and ancient Jewish community. At first the governor of Majorca offered his hospitality to the Jews in his fortress. About eight hundred found refuge there, but three hundred who remained outside were killed. Others succeeded in escaping by boat to Africa. The community of Ibiza was annihilated. News of the effective pogroms in Majorca reached Barcelona. On the Sabbath of the first week in August 1391, one hundred Jews were killed there. The real massacre began the following Monday.

The litany of misery, torture and bloodshed is endless. It occurred in every Spanish town. In a letter to the community of Avignon, the philosopher Rabbi Hasdai Crescas describes graphically the events he witnessed during those terrible months. His account is of particular interest because it tells of the emergence of an utterly new Jewish phenomenon in the midst of the familiar bloodshed and suffering. In his description we witness, for the first time in Jewish history, the large-scale conversion of the Jews. The letter is dated Saragossa, October 19, 1391:

If I were to tell you here all the numerous sufferings we have endured, you would be dumbfounded at the thought of them; I will therefore set before you only in brief detail the table of our disaster set with poisonous plant and wormwood, giving you a bare recital of the fact so that you may satiate yourselves on the bitterness of our wormwood and drink from the wine of our grief. As I suppose that you have been told the story already, I will recount it as briefly as possible, commencing as follows:

On the day of the New Moon of the fateful month of Tammus in the year 5151 [1391], the Lord bent the bow of his enemies against the populous community of Seville where there were between 6,000 and 7,000 heads of families, and they destroyed their gates by fire and killed in that very place a great number of people; the majority, however, changed their faith. Many of them, children as well as women, were sold to the Moslems, so that the streets occupied by Jews have become empty. Many of them, sanctifying the Holy Name, endured death, but many also broke the holy covenant.

From there the fire spread and consumed all the cedars of Lebanon [Jews] in the holy community of the city of Cordoba. Here, too, many changed their faith, and the community became desolate.

. . . [in] the community of Toledo, and in the Temple of the Lord, the priests and the learned were murdered. The rabbis, the descendants of the virtuous and excellent R. Asher of blessed memory, together with their children and pupils, publicly sanctified the Holy Name. However, many who had not the courage to save their souls changed their faith here too.

. . . On the 7th of Ab the Lord destroyed the community of Valencia in which there were about a thousand heads of families; about two hundred and fifty men died, sanctifying the name of the Lord, the others fled into the mountain; some of these saved themselves, but the majority changed their faith.

... the community of Barcelona ... was destroyed ... The number of murdered amounted to two hundred and fifty souls; the rest fled into the castle where they were saved. The enemies plundered all streets inhabited by Jews ... and even set fire to some of them. The authorities of the province, however, took no part in this; instead they endeavored to protect the Jews ... and even set about punishing the wrongdoers, when a furious mob rose against the better classes in the country and fought against the Jews who were in the castle, with bows and missiles, and killed them in the castle itself. Amongst the many who sanctified the name of the Lord was my only son, whom I have offered as a faultless lamb for the sacrifice. . . . Many . . . slaughtered themselves. . . . Many also came forth and sanctified the name of the Lord in the open street. All the others changed their faith and only a few found refuge in the towns of the princes. . . . however, these were precisely the most esteemed. Consequently ... there is none left in Barcelona today who still bears the name of Jew.

The *converso* had appeared and he was unique in Jewish history. There had been virtually no converts from anti-Jewish riots in the Middle Ages. In the rest of Europe, Jews were murdered or they committed suicide rather than become Christians. All previous attempts to convert Jews during the Middle Ages in other parts of the world had been, for the Church, dismal failures. In Mainz, during the Crusades, an observer wrote: "Twelve thousand Jews were roasted to such a degree that the window leading and the bells of the Church of St. Quirinis were melted. In Eislingen, rather than convert, the whole Jewish community gathered in their wooden synagogue and set it on fire. In Frankfurt, they set fire to their own houses and threw themselves into the flames." An eyewitness watched thirty-eight Jews perish during the Crusades and wrote: "How stubborn the Jews are. I should find it difficult to believe if I had not seen it with my own eyes, how they not only sang and laughed as they burned, but many of them leaped and exulted and suffered death with great firmness despite the torture which they were evidently undergoing." However, in Spain, where a comparatively small number were killed, many chose conversion. Comparatively few "sanctified the Holy Name." Many more embraced the Cross.

It is reported by reliable contemporary historians that within less than ten years, more than two hundred thousand Spanish Jews were converted. The number grew as the zeal of the Catholic Church increased and leading Jews—lay leaders and even some rabbis—accepted the faith with even greater fervor than the converting priests. In some instances, whole communities were baptized. In Valencia, for instance, all the survivors of the massacre converted.

Only a small minority of those who lived through the slaughter returned to their communities and rebuilt their synagogues. The majority, however, was anxious to accept Christianity. "They came forward demanding baptism in such droves," writes a chronicler of these events, "that in all the churches the holy chrism was exhausted and the priests knew not where to get more [baptismal oil]. But each morning the Chrismatory would be found miraculously filled so that the supply held out, nor was this by any means the only sign that the whole terrible affair was the mysterious work of Providence to effect a holy end."

Apocryphal as this story undoubtedly is, it bears a striking resemblance to the Jewish legend of the sanctification of the Temple in Jerusalem in the second century B.C. The Temple had been contaminated by Syrian pagans. When the Jews, led by the hero Judas Maccabeus, overthrew the

tyranny of the Syrians, they went to the Temple to rededi-
cate it. Only a small supply of holy oil was left. But here,
too, it was miraculously replenished for the eight days it
took to cleanse the sanctuary. The Jews commemorate this
miracle during the feast of lights, Hanukkah, when eight
candles are lit on successive days in Jewish homes.

The eagerness of the Spanish Jews to convert was both a
disgrace and an enigma which tortured contemporaries and
haunted the Jews for generations even after the expulsion.
Ibn Lehamias Alami, a Jewish moralist of the early fifteenth
century, rather than accuse the Church, denounces his own
people. Both death and conversion were to him divine punishment for the sins of the Spanish Jews:

> Because we had striven to dress like the Gentiles, we have
> been forced instead to wear some strange clothing so that we
> should be singled out for shame and contempt before the on-
> looking public. Because we had despoiled our beard and hair-
> dos, we have been ordered to grow our hair long and to wear
> beards like mourners. Because, oblivious of the destruction of
> the Temple we have built spacious and beautiful mansions and
> palaces, we have been expelled and driven into the open fields
> and slum-like corners.

Hidden within the theological notions of reward and
punishment, concealed behind these pious words, we can
find the reality behind the mass conversions, for the on-
slaught of the Spanish mob, its furor and its passions, cannot have been greater than that of the crusaders or the
rabble that stormed the ghettos of Frankfurt and other
European communities. The massacres of Seville and Toledo were not more violent or bloody than the Russian
pogroms. In other parts of Europe the occasional converts
to Christianity were treated as rare exceptions. In Spain it

was those who withstood baptism who were unique, and the number of New Christians was soon so great that they set the tone for the whole community.

Parallels are dangerous tools of history; they are at best illustrations. But we can find one example of Jewish conversion to Christianity which may be compared to the *converso* phenomenon. In the nineteenth century an estimated one hundred and twenty thousand Jews converted in Western Europe less than a century following their emancipation by the French Revolution. To be sure, even then there were no mass conversions. Nowhere did whole communities succumb, but whole families did, and an astoundingly large number of individuals realized how much easier it would be to live as Christians in a Christian society rather than swim upstream. Heinrich Heine, the German poet who was himself a convert, said flippantly that his baptism was really not a religious act at all but "the admission ticket to Western civilization." He considered himself the "blank page between the Old and the New Testament." Conversion was a marriage of convenience to a society which had not yet fully recovered from medieval prejudice, though these converts were not forced to convert because of massacres or pogroms. Nor was the Christian faith of the nineteenth century as serious as the Catholicism of fifteenth-century Spain. It was the religion of the majority, but it was rarely as intimately connected with the political and military power structure of the country as it was in Spain. The nineteenth century produced millions of nonbelievers, even among those who had always belonged to the Church. And for the Jews who converted to Christianity, their new faith was often as unserious as their Jewish convictions had been.

The similarity between these two groups of Jews who lived centuries apart lies in the fact that both lived in relative freedom, a privilege not often granted to Jews. As we have seen, the Spanish Jews were almost totally free for many centuries. The term "Golden Era"—used for the period of great Jewish activity which saw the writings of Yehuda Halevi, the poet; Solomon Ibn Gabirol, the theologian; and Ibn Ezra, the Biblical commentator—was also an era of material affluence and influence. The Jews had rights and even power in the highest circles of society. The castles that were often placed at the disposal of the Jewish community during that time present a striking contrast to the ghettos and *shtetls* in which European Jews were forced to live. The prosperity of the large Spanish Jewish community, many of whose members converted during the fourteenth century, had no parallel in any other country at that time. Similarly, the Jews of nineteenth-century Western Europe converted only after laws of equality had permitted them to attain wealth and power, and granted them access to a society from which they had been cut off for centuries.

The Jews, as a people, have learned to survive adversity. Until this very day they have not learned how to survive— as Jews—in freedom. Whenever they have been at liberty to choose whether or not to be Jews, they have yielded to some degree. Of course, this has not always meant outright conversion. Often it has just resulted in a weakening of the specifically Jewish fiber of survival. They simply assimilate, in many ways, to the culture of the country in which they live and become "like the other nations of the world." In traditional Jewish thought this has always been considered a curse. Many Jewish laws, such as the dietary restrictions, have their origin in an attempt at the preservation of the uniqueness of the Jewish people. They were meant to isolate the Jews from the customs and cultures of the people among whom they lived. Creative Jewish continuity, as well as physical survival, was the real goal of these admonitions. In freedom the temptations to move away from the strict observances of old customs have always been very great.

So the walls of the ghettos of Central and Eastern Europe served not only to isolate the Jews but to preserve their Jewishness. In this closely knit society the strict laws of moral conduct were administered by Jewish lay authorities, and the rabbis saw to it that the rituals and beliefs of the Jewish faith were observed. This provided enough Jewish substance to meet all challenges. The ghetto walls separated the Jews from the affluence of the Christian world, but within them, Jewish spiritual life prospered. The average ghetto Jew felt comfort and happiness in his Jewish existence and did not complain about the difficult restrictions imposed upon him by the Christian community. In his eyes there was not really so much to envy in the Christian world. The material wealth he saw was not great and it was in the hands of a very few. In addition, his Jewish heritage had taught him that "the ignorant cannot be pious," and so, confronted with illiterate Christians who had to recite their prayers by rote, the Jew, who spent his days with books, experienced a sense of superiority which strengthened him. The "heroism" and stamina of the ghetto Jew who preferred death to conversion was derived from no more mysterious source than his deep religious conviction and a strict adherence to his ancient tradition, which made conversion an unthinkable alternative.

In Spain the Jews' close contact with the general community under the reign of the Muslims, and later under the Christian kings, made for laxity and indifference toward their Jewish heritage. Jews ate at the tables of the Spanish grandees without thinking of the dietary restrictions. Although intermarriage was out of the question, close and intimate relationships between Jews and Christian Spaniards were not rare. Only after the bitter experience of the massacres of 1391 did the rabbis remember to admonish the Jewish community and to remind them that the ancient laws must be observed. The *conversos* were lost to their faith, but the little remnant of believing Jews who lived in the rebuilt *juderías* had to be brought closer to the "fountain of faith." All those who disobeyed the Jewish ritual were to be punished. Nonobservance became a criminal offense. In the minds of those who had resisted the temptation of conversion there was the deep belief that it was a lack of Jewish tradition which had brought about the disgrace of the *conversos*.

But these rabbinical admonitions came too late for the majority of the Jewish community. If they had been issued a century earlier, such disciplinary cautions might have served to protect the Jews from conversion. In retrospect, they were only a remarkable documentation of the causes for the downfall of Spanish Jewry:

Considering that everything depends on the worship of the Creator, that the evil decrees came upon the world because of the sins of the generation and that the preservation of the communities depends upon their good deeds—this has been true in the case of all past generations and is doubly so in that of our generation, when on account of our sins, we have remained but a few in lieu of many—we need to mend our ways and to set up fences and regulations concerning the service of the

Creator as the service of our Lord the King, so that we may continue to live in the realm.

Whatever the motivation or cause for the mass conversions in Spain, the true results were soon discovered. Many of those who had been lukewarm Jews had become indifferent Christians. Having paid mere lip service to the religion of their fathers, they were bound to have little respect for their new faith. Of course there were some genuine conversions, but the great majority of the *conversos* did not become faithful Christians, although they managed to look like enthusiastic disciples. They were meticulous in their public Christian behavior: they attended the service in the cathedral, they carried rosaries instead of prayer shawls, they recited "Ave Marias" instead of "Hear O Israel," they joined in the processions, and as might be expected, their donations to the churches were conspicuously generous. But if the Christians, seeing these external manifestations of the piety of their proselytes, thought that they had won fervent new worshipers and believers for their Church, they were sadly mistaken. If they thought conversion would solve the problems of too great a Jewish influence in high places, they were soon to see that they had committed a tragic blunder.

It is true that the Jews, besides changing their names and places of residence, married into the families of nobles; they even entered the priesthood. But they did not yield their social position or their economic influence. Within twenty years the *conversos* had become, to the Christian community, the major problem of Spanish life. Vincent Ferrer, the priest who had devoted his life to the conversion of the Jews and who had been beatified for the success of his forcible baptisms of the Jewish community, had, in fact, been honored for failure. He and all the other fanatical preachers had only succeeded in diluting the Christian faith and burdening Spain with the almost insoluble problem of make-believe Christians. The Church, in the end, had to resort to even sterner methods to rid itself of the false converts than those it had employed to force the conversions. And the New Christians became a problem to themselves. After a time the schizophrenic nature of their lives was discernible even to the man in the street. It became a badge of honor to be able to say, "I am an Old Christian." It meant "I am of pure blood." It was then that the New Christians, particularly those who had not rid themselves of the memory of their Jewish heritage, were given the contemptuous new name, Marranos—swine. The word articulated not only the hatred of the populace for the false Christians, it also carried over the envy they had historically felt toward the prosperity of the practicing Jew.

The Church, which had tolerated, and the state, which had encouraged, Jewish financiers, physicians, tax collectors, councillors of the state and intimates of the kings, now made it possible for the New Christians to climb even higher. The conversions, so obviously superficial and perfunctory, had created an almost comical situation. *Conversos* became the symbols of successful Christian conquest and were soon sought after by the nobility, which at one time might have hesitated to invite Jews, however highly placed, into their homes. Now every nobleman seemed to have "his *converso*." The Marrano became the center and the pride of Spanish social life. The Spanish Jewish intellectuals, who had always been known for their wit and sarcasm, could now be invited into noble homes without fear of risking the bishop's displeasure. With their new Christian identities, the Jews were not merely acceptable, their baptism made them sought after in high Spanish society. Their role was similar to that of prominent blacks who were invited into the homes of wealthy liberals in the early days of the American civil rights movement.

The financial and social success of the Marranos was miraculous. They had "conquered" Spain from within.

At the end of the fifteenth century the entire administration of Aragon was in Converso hands; at the very moment the Inquisition began to function, five conversos—Luis Santangel, Gabriel Sanches, Sanche de Paternoy, Felipe Climent and Alfonso de la Caballeria—held the five most important posts in the kingdom. Sons and grandsons of Conversos continued this predominance. . . . The persistence of Conversos in Spanish life . . . may be explained by the fact that so many of the leading families of the realm contained Converso blood that it would have been impossible to ignore talented members from them. What nobody can doubt is that Converso contribution was out of all proportion to their members. The names of Fernando de Rojas, author of the drama "Celestina"; the great humanist Luis Vives; the blessed Juan de Ávila; Luis de Leon; and St. Theresa of Ávila are only a beginning to the list of hundreds of likely and unlikely Conversos whose names have illuminated not simply Spanish but the whole of Western European history.

Although it is impossible to obtain reliable statistical information, it has been estimated that the total number of New Christians never exceeded a quarter of a million. But since the vast majority of the Spaniards were illiterate and the somewhat less illiterate nobility were without great ambition, a quarter of a million people of the caliber of the Spanish Jews were bound to have a disproportionate influence on the population.

From the Spanish point of view, the most insidious of the Marrano successes was their invasion of the Church itself. Marranos became not only monks and nuns and parish priests; they also rose to high Church position and became bishops and cardinals. Rabbi Solomon Halevi was one of the sincere converts to Christianity who found his new vocation in the Church. He became, after his conversion, the Bishop of Burgos. Bartolomeo Carranza, Archbishop of Toledo and Primate of Spain, and Hernando de Talavera, Archbishop of Granada, were two other outstanding clergymen who were New Christians.

The monasteries were considered particularly safe refuges for *conversos,* and the Society of Jesus, which was founded in the sixteenth century by St. Ignatius of Loyola, included many monks of Jewish descent. Ignatius himself had been suspected of observing Jewish customs in secret. The accusation was a nonsensical fabrication, but it is said that Ignatius was proud to have been accused of being a close relative of Jesus and the Holy Mother Mary. He was so utterly free of anti-Jewish feeling that he appointed Diego Lainex, a man known to have been born a Jew, to succeed him.

The list of New Christian clergymen of the highest ranks, not to speak of simple monks and priests, is too long to be mentioned here. Probably the most remarkable case is that of St. Theresa of Ávila, the greatest of Christian women mystics, known as the *"compatrona d'España,"* the patron saint of Spain; she was a converted Jew. Some of the most fervent of the *conversos* proved their loyalty to the Church some years later by becoming the most vigorous and brutal of the Grand Inquisitors. The most notorious of these is Tomás de Torquemada, who was descended from a Jewish family, as was his equally violent assistant, Diego de Deza.

But others who entered the priesthood were Christians in name only. Like so many of their fellow *conversos,* they had developed a strange habit: they practiced Judaism in secret. They were Judaizers. (In Portugal, almost two hundred years after the conversion of their ancestors, forty-four nuns, seven canons and eight priests were burned at the stake for Judaizing.) Judaizing became so widespread among the *conversos* that it soon was the great issue of the time. At first some of the Marranos did not think it necessary to hide their heresy. As it became more dangerous, Jewish ritual was practiced under many safeguards. All the same, there were many contemporary witnesses to the secret Jewish practices of the Marranos.

These heretics [says Cura de Los Palacios] avoid baptizing their children and, when they could not prevent it, they washed off the baptismal water after they returned home from the church. They eat meat on [Christian] fast days and unleavened bread on Passover, which they observe as well as the Sabbath; they have Jews who secretly preach in their houses and rabbis who slaughter meat and fowl for them; they perform all Jewish ceremonies in secret as well as they can and avoid, as far as possible, receiving the sacrament; they never confess truly. A confessor, after hearing one of them, cut off a corner of his garment saying: "Since you have never sinned, I want a piece of your garment as a relic to cure the sick." They assumed airs of superiority, asserting that there was no better race on earth, nor wiser, nor shrewder, nor more honorable through their descent from the tribes of Israel.

In the *Shevet Yehudah,* a play by the Jewish writer Solomon Ibn Verga, a Christian relates a conversation between an Inquisitor of Seville and a Duke. The Inquisitor admits how hopeless his task is of eliminating Jewish practices from the households of the "Christian Marranos." "If you wish, Sire, to know how the Marranos observe the Sabbath, let us go up to the Tower." On the tower, the Inquisitor tells the Duke:

Raise your eyes and see. That house there is the house of a Marrano, so is the other, and many others. Despite the hard winter you will not see smoke coming out of any of them, for they have failed to make a fire on account of the Sabbath. We also have been told about one particular Marrano in Spain who ate unleavened bread all year so that he could consume it on Passover without raising suspicion; he claimed that his stomach could not tolerate leavened bread. On holidays when the blowing of the horn is prescribed, they go out in to the open country, and in the midst of the mountains and valleys they blow the horn without being overheard by outsiders.

They have a man who clandestinely circumcises them. There are some individuals who circumcise themselves, for they rely on no other man for fear he might divulge the act. Some bring with them the scrolls of the Laws of Moses in sacks of pepper and similar things with the other commandments. It is of no use to Your Majesty to pour Holy water on Jews and to call them Peter or Paul, while they adhere to their religion like Akiba or Tarphon. There is no advantage in their baptism except to make them overweening against true Christians and without fear, since outwardly they are accepted as Christians. The royal tribute which they used to pay when they were Jews they pay no more. Know, Sire, that Judaism is no doubt one of the incurable diseases.

This was certainly a graphic way to put the situation so that it would have the greatest impact on a medieval audience. To the ears of the medieval listener, a survivor, no doubt of several of the plagues which periodically killed whole populations, "incurable diseases" were a more threatening reality than they are today when there is hope for new cures and most epidemic diseases have been eliminated. In the Middle Ages, "incurable" meant just that. No remedy was in sight. Yet both church and state were searching for a cure for the new disease which had already reached epidemic proportions. The symptoms were Christians without Christianity, worshipers without piety. Judaizing had to be attacked, if only to pacify the ordinary man, to whom Judaizing Christians were a mockery of the true religion.

But there was more to it than that. Spain had declared the "reconquest" a success. Except for a stronghold in Granada, the country was free of its Moorish infidels, and hundreds of thousands of Jews had converted. This made the realization that the Jews had "invaded" Spain from within seem an unbearable outrage. It made a mockery of the holy passions of the converters who had stormed the synagogues with crucifixes held high like banners or swords. Judaism was not only incurable, it seemed to be invincible. Conversion, clearly, had simply forced the Jews to change their names, but it allowed them to live in the most luxurious mansions and had even freed them of the special taxes which were still being collected from those Jews who had resisted the temptation to convert. Rather than solving the "Jewish question," the mass conversions had created a new problem: a powerful middle-class made up of secret Jews.

Almost a century had elapsed since the great massacres of 1391 during which Spain had admitted a quarter of a million Jews into the Church. For nearly three generations these New Christians had lived their strange lives of memories, nostalgia and conflict. Many of them no longer remembered their former existence as Jews and had been fully integrated into Spanish life, church and nation. But those who had never freed themselves of their Jewish past and secretly practiced Jewish customs were now considered Christian heretics by the Church they had adopted.

The incurable disease had to be cured. The remedy that was chosen isolated Spain from the great new movements of humanism and the Renaissance which were beginning to blossom in much of Europe. While Italy shone in the splendor of a new creativity, Spain renewed one of the cruelest aspects of the Middle Ages. In contrast to the Renaissance, which was opening the eyes of mankind to new vistas of free inquiry and a new critical approach to religious dogma, Spain reverted to a form of religious torment which dated back to the thirteenth century. While the popes in Rome, who might have intervened to prevent the tragedy that followed, looked on passively, Ferdinand and Isabella called for the re-establishment of the Inquisition to ferret out the new infidels and heretics who had invaded the Church.

Heresy had been a problem for the Church since the early Middle Ages. Ironically, it was the Crusades, during which the Christians were exposed to many strange outside influences, that encouraged the flourishing of religious deviates. The Church began to deal seriously with this problem in the twelfth century, during the reign of one of the most orthodox and rigid popes, Innocent III. Then, at the Fourth Lateran Council, in 1215, the battle against the Albigensian and Athanasian heresies began. It was carried out by the Dominican Order of Monks, and the instrument through which they made their inquiries into these heresies was known as the Office of the Inquisition. It had its own rules of procedure and its own system of torture and punishment, the climax of which was the auto-da-fé, a public hearing at which suspected heretics were either reconciled to the Church or sentenced to death by fire. The executions were then carried out while the screams of the victims were drowned out by the jubilation of the mob assembled by the thousands for the performances. The Spanish rulers of the fifteenth century had only to call for the re-establishment of this old institution which would provide them with a weapon against the heretics of their day, the Marranos.

The first of the new inquisitional tribunals was established in Seville in 1478, but it was not until 1480 that it began to function. By 1482 the Inquisition had been expanded, with new Inquisitors appointed and new cities added. It was at this point that Tomás de Torquemada, the queen's fanatical confessor, whose name has become synonymous with the word "Inquisitor," came to power.

The Inquisition is considered one of the many traumatic experiences of Jewish history, and as such, it is always spoken of with dread. But, of course, the Inquisition had no power over Jews at all. It was established for the purpose of dealing with Christians who had deviated from their faith. The Marranos who were called to account for their secret practices appeared not as Jews but as allegedly heretical Christians. The number of Marranos who were executed in this particularly barbaric way is estimated at approximately thirty thousand. The same Inquisition also punished Muslims who were uncommitted Christian converts. Many of these Moriscos, as they were called, perished along with Marranos during the Inquisition's time of power. However, no unconverted Jews were ever called to the tribunals.

An important factor, both for the vigorous prosecution of the Marranos and the severity of the sentences they received, was the deep-seated and widespread anti-Jewish, anti-Marrano sentiments of the Spanish people and the courts. The tribunals depended heavily on informers and had little trouble finding them in the cities, like Seville, which had large Marrano communities. The system of secret police which invited informers, spies and eavesdroppers subjected the whole society to a climate of suspicion which often proved unfounded or was based on the slightest "evidence."

Henry C. Lea, the great historian of the Inquisition, provides us with some examples of the sort of testimony which was enough to convict accused Marranos during this time:

Changing the body linen or table linen on Saturday, lighting candles on Friday and similar observances were proofs of a most damaging character; even eating amin—a broth liked by Jews—enumerated among the offenses entailing appearance in an auto-da-fé. When Brianda de Bardaxi was on trial at Saragossa in 1491, she admitted that, when a child, she had eaten a few mouthfuls of Passover bread given her by a playmate, and this was gravely detailed in her sentence as one of the proofs of "vehement suspicion" for which she was severely punished. Circumcision . . . was an evidence almost decisive and, with male defendants, an inspection by the surgeon of the tribunal was customary; but in an earlier time, before the expulsion and forced conversion of the Jews, it was merely an indication that a man was a New, not an Old, Christian, yet in an auto-da-fé at Saragossa in 1486, Pedro and Luis de Almazán, on this evidence alone, were sentenced to perform penance with lighted candles and to ten years of exile. . . . a propensity to cleanliness by washing oneself was an indication of apostasy, and in the trial of Marie Gómez at Toledo, in 1550, as a relapsed impenitent, one of the charges was that, in her former trial she had not confessed that, some fifteen years before, a kid had been killed at her house by cutting its throat.

How slander was the evidence requisite for prosecution is manifested in the trials of a whole family in Valladolid. When Dr. Jorge Enriques, physician to the Duke of Alva, died, the body was soiled, requiring washing, followed by a clean shirt. A number of witnesses thereupon deposed that it was prepared for sepulture according to Jewish rites . . . So in 1625, Manuel de Azvedo, a shoemaker of Salamanca, was denounced because he had removed a lump of fat from the leg of mutton which he took to a baker to be roasted. . . . Azvedo said he was ignorant of this being a Jewish custom but had been told that a leg of mutton roasted better with the fat cut out. . . . he proved he was an Old Christian on all sides; he was not acquitted but the case was suspended. . . . In another case one of the charges was that the accused in slicing bread held the knife with the edge turned away and not towards his breast as was customary with Christians. Trivial as all this may seem, one occasionally meets a case showing that the Inquisition did not always spend its energies in vain following up the slenderest evidence. In several cases in Valladolid, the chief evidence was that the meat before cooking was soaked in water to remove blood and grease. This led to the discovery and punishment as Judaizers of a group of some fifteen or twenty Benavente, who appeared in the auto-da-fé. As soon as one was brought in, he implicated others and the net was spread which captured them all. The fact, however, that torture was freely used casts an unpleasant doubt over the justice of the result.

The auto-da-fé was the culmination of a long process of suspicion, arrest, investigation, torture and long imprisonment. These preliminaries, sometimes extending over periods of many years, were often as difficult to endure as death itself. Not everyone was, in fact, sentenced to die, only those who refused to admit heresy. In the majority of cases, prolonged imprisonment in jails which defy description, and a thousand indignities and humiliations, were just the prelude to a lesser but still severe punishment: exclusion from society and confiscation of the prisoner's possessions. Those who were fortunate enough to escape the pyre found themselves in useless freedom, stripped of all their possessions and incapable of finding employment. If they were lucky they had friends who had escaped the Inquisition, but often the person who befriended a former prisoner became the object of suspicion and was himself arrested.

As at the opening of the bullfight season in the great arenas of Madrid, the dignitaries of city and state were seated on decorated balconies, surrounded by members of the nobility, both men and women, and the highest clergy. There were processions of church officials who carried sacred objects to the site. But the highlight of the preliminaries was the entrance of the accused wearing the garments of penitence, the sanbenito. Usually made of yellow cloth, these sleeveless, open-sided robes were decorated with crosses and the name and the sins of the culprit. Those who were condemned to death wore black sanbenitos ornamented with flames and devils. After the burning, the sanbenitos belonging to the executed heretics were not so easily discarded. They were usually hung in the church as a way of warning people to shun the families. At times, the wearing of the sanbenito became a form of punishment for those who were not executed. Along with the other penances exacted from the accused, the prolonged wearing of the sanbenito was proof of the former heretic's devotion to the Church, the "act of faith" which was the goal of the auto-da-fé.

Although there are several engravings of autos-da-fé, they

convey nothing of the horrors of these elaborate public exhibitions of human inhumanity. And in El Greco's famous portrait of the Grand Inquisitor, Fernando Neno de Guevara, we cannot find any evidence of this shameful spectacle in the face we see. El Greco depicts a man of noble splendor, both in dress and demeanor. His dark eyes behind dark-rimmed spectacles, his thin lips and his stern look bespeak only great dignity and sincerity. If this man was the head of a pious murder scheme, his portrait certainly does not show it. In actual fact, although the ecclesiastical court pronounced the judgment with due dignity, it protected itself against self-accusation and collective guilt by what we would call a technicality. The execution itself was left to the state. The Grand Inquisitor, servant of the Church, did not actually murder. He only recommended it to the less vulnerable authorities.

Moreover, if it was piety and deep religious conviction which motivated the men of the Inquisition, it was a religious faith which paid handsomely. Every conviction meant not simply heretics punished or reconciled but fortunes confiscated. And the proceeds filled not only the coffers of the state but the treasures of the Grand Inquisitors as well. It was common knowledge that the arrests and condemnations of so many Marranos were not merely undertaken for religious purification of these supposed heretics. The income derived from the judgment, whether the sentence was death or the result reconciliation, was enormous. Many multimillionaires, even by today's standards, either died at the stake or in dungeons. Others were released with minor punishment. But no matter what the verdict, confiscation of property was a foregone conclusion. The accused all left the high tribunal as beggars. Perhaps this explains why the

Inquisition, called out of the past in the 1480s, maintained itself well into the nineteenth century.

In view of the virulent anti-Jewish, anti-Marrano feelings both in the Church and among the people, it is not surprising that the burghers and common people, as well as the nobles and the clergy, watched the proceedings and the success of the Inquisition with great interest and satisfaction. What is amazing is the reaction of the unconverted Jew. While the Marranos understandably lived in fear of being denounced by their servants, their friends, even their children, the Jews felt safe, if not a bit smug. Because they had their own reasons for disdaining the Marranos, they shared the Christians' contempt for the neophytes. After all, not all of the Marranos had been forced to convert; some of them had left Judaism voluntarily. And the Jews still lived restricted lives, while the Marranos were permitted to live outside the *juderías* and were free of Jewish taxes. If the Marranos felt a snobbish sense of superiority toward the unconverted Jews, the Jews' attitude toward the Marranos certainly contained envy and perhaps a bit of self-hatred.

The tragic short-sightedness of the Spanish-Jewish attitude toward the Inquisition, so apparent to us today, occurred to none of the Jewish observers of that time. None of them seemed to understand that the trials against former Jews must have been stimulated by venomous hatreds which threatened believing Jews as well as Marrano heretics. Only a decade after the reconstitution of the Inquisition, the Jews were expelled from Spain by royal decree. Few of the Jews who lived through the Inquisition saw it as a prelude to the end of the long history of their people in Spain. It was, in fact, at the royal palace itself that they felt they had found clear proof that their trust in the king's friendship was justified.

Like his predecessors on the throne of Spain, Ferdinand surrounded himself with intimate Jewish advisers. Riba Altes was his personal physician; Luis de Santanal was one of the richest and most powerful men in the country; and Abraham Senior, who was also the official head of the Spanish-Jewish community, was the king's most trusted councillor of state. This was not all. Practically the whole royal household was of Jewish descent, many of them just one generation removed from their Jewish origins, known as Marranos to everyone in the realm. Isabella had selected as her confessor Herando de Talavera, although she knew that his mother was a Jew. Also, Pedro de la Caballería, a very recent *converso*, had arranged the wedding of the two monarchs. When the arrangements were completed, Abraham Senior and Don Solomon of Aragon presented Isabella with a magnificent golden necklace bought with money that had been raised by Jews. Many years later when the queen died, it was the Marquesa de Moya, a member of a *converso* family and wife of the king's private chamberlain, who closed the queen's eyes.

But the best proof of the Jews' security was the appearance in 1484 of the most outstanding Jew of his time, Don Isaac Abravanel, whose father had already held the highest position in his native Portugal as financier of Prince Fernando, son of King João. His grandfather and great-grandfather had also been treasurers and financiers of the royal household of Portugal. Don Isaac had inherited many millions of maravidas from his family and had added many more himself. Yet he was not merely a millionaire and a financial genius, he was a Jewish scholar of note and a distinguished statesman. That he was received by Ferdinand and Isabella was a sure sign that all was serene in the Jewish community. With so much protection and such influential friends at court, what could happen to them?

But even as Abravanel negotiated with the king, the plan for the total expulsion of the Jews had been decided upon. It happened that at that time the Spanish army was engaged in the final struggle against the Moors, the battle for Granada. A great deal of money was needed and if a Jew of Abravanel's financial genius could provide it, why not postpone the expulsion of his people until a more propitious moment? That even Abravanel, a man of extraordinary political experience and acumen, could mistake a polite and cordial reception by the monarchs for assurance of his people's security seems incomprehensible. But it is consistent with the experience and attitude of Jews throughout their history.

In any attempt at defining their specific psyche or "mystique," we must include that most puzzling and yet most revealing contradiction in the Jewish mentality: the apparent inability of the Jews to understand or predict their own catastrophes. The Jews, whose history consists of one tragedy after another, have yet to be prepared for any one of them. Clemenceau, who as a young man witnessed the most notorious of anti-Jewish trials, the affair of Alfred Dreyfus, is supposed to have remarked that "only the defendant did not understand" the Jewish implications of the trial. It can safely be said that the only ones who were oblivious to the possibility of their own destruction in fifteenth-century Spain were the Jews. So they surrendered, died or lost their fortunes, and those who survived were finally expelled from the land of their birth.

This sort of blindness has been true throughout Jewish history. Jews have always been the last to know what everyone else could have predicted. It is as if they simply do not believe it possible. In the Middle Ages they were expelled from England, France and many of the German states. As far as they were concerned, it "happened overnight." They packed up and left. But nothing really happens "overnight."

In Vienna, after the Thirty Years' War, for example, the wealth of many of the Jewish families intoxicated the whole Jewish community, and the fact that a few families were even knighted seemed assurance of a safe existence. In 1670, because the queen of Austria suffered several miscarriages, the whole Jewish community was expelled. It was predictable that the anti-Semitism of the large majority of Viennese society would make the Jews easy and natural scapegoats. However, it came as a shock to the Jews. In Russia, some Jews seemed to prosper during the Thirty Years' War because they were the tax collectors for the state. They did not seem to realize that this was a hazardous occupation for a minority community. They were oblivious to the feelings against them which were growing among the poor, the peasants, the illiterate. In 1648, half a million Jews died in a single pogrom led by a peasant Cossack. They were unprepared for this event; nor did they foresee the pogroms in Russia which were stimulated by the outrageous laws of May 1881 creating a special Pale of Settlement. No major voluntary emigration by Russian Jews followed the promulgation of these laws. And twenty years later, only a relatively small percentage of Jews left. The majority stayed on.

The most tragic example of this Jewish readiness to play

the role of the eternal victim occurred during the Hitler regime. There was a full decade between Hitler's *Putsch* in Munich and his advent to power. Only a handful of German Jews were apprehensive. Hardly a Jew took him seriously. The Jewish intellectuals ridiculed him. The average German-Jewish patriotic burgher discounted him as an Austrian foreigner. When he finally became Chancellor, the Jews were calling it an "episode" which would soon pass. It took Hitler from 1933 to 1939 to decide on the "final solution" to the Jewish problem, the extermination of the Jews. The German Jews had five years during which they could have escaped. Only forty percent did.

This form of political naïveté and blindness must be considered as one of the characteristics of the Jewish collective unconscious. The Jewish people are optimists, addicted to a passionate belief that they cannot possibly have enemies bent on their destruction. Restrictions may be part of their daily lives, but destruction, they believe, is utterly impossible. Much of this optimism is reflected in Jewish wit. But basic to this psychological quirk is another, more serious component of the Jewish mentality. The Jews seem to have a perverse talent for developing an unhappy and totally uncritical patriotism for the countries in which they live. They were Frenchmen who adored the tricolor when, during the days of Dreyfus, the streets of Paris were full of mobs yelling "*À bas les juifs!*" They were loyal Germans and faithful Englishmen, and loving children of Russia, in spite of the storm troopers, degradation and pogroms. And by 1492 they had been Spaniards for centuries.

That is why the Spanish Jews were caught by surprise when the edict expelling them was proclaimed to the jubilation of all of Christian Spain. They had lived in the country since long before Christ. They were not foreigners. Many of them had even become New Christians only in order to appear to be more Spanish. It is part of the Marrano phenomenon that they did not merely embrace the Cross; their conversion, in many cases, was a kiss to the country as well. Yet the country continued to consider them unwelcome strangers.

The collective scene of the summer months of 1492, following the order for expulsion, has been compassionately described by Andrés Bernáldez:

> Trusting in the vain hopes of their blindness, they chose the hardships of the road and they left the land of their birth, small and big, old men and children, on foot or riding asses and other beasts and on carts, travelling to the ports from which they were to sail, and they went along the road or across the fields with great hardship and risks, some falling, some rising, some dying, some being born and some falling sick. . . . Their rabbis kept encouraging them and they made the women and their youngsters sing and play the tambourines to cheer the crowd.

They had not made plans concerning their belongings, and most of them left everything behind. Some eighty thousand succeeded in getting across the border to Portugal. (It was just as safe for them as Holland was, four centuries later, for the parents of Anne Frank. Within a few years the Inquisition reached into Portugal.) About ten thousand went by ship to North Africa, Italy, Turkey. Most of them never reached their destinations. Sometimes the flimsy ships were wrecked by storm. In some cases the captains robbed them of the little money, gold and jewels they had managed to hide.

Many of them, about fifty thousand, remained in Spain, swelling the number of Marranos. A hundred years after the massacre of 1391 these people, whose ancestors had survived the pogroms of Seville and Toledo and had remained faithful to the heritage of their people, finally let go of their faith. Unlike their fellow Jews who had to sell a house for a donkey or a field for a piece of cloth in order to flee the country, these New Christians had only to surrender their religious beliefs to find freedom.

There were many, of course, who became new Marranos —new Judaizers—creating new problems and posing new challenges for the Spanish authorities. Before their conversion the new Marranos had seen what the Inquisition could do. They had felt the effects of anti-Jewish feelings among the people. Now they were eager to convert. Among the first was Abraham Senior, the king's councillor. With his whole family he assumed the name of Coronel and became a Christian. The monarchs waited in vain for Don Isaac Abravanel to follow suit. He chose to leave the country instead.

The year 1492 had been a year of great triumph for the Spanish nation. Granada, the last Moorish stronghold, was conquered, and much of the credit for the victory went to the queen, who visited the battlefield to bolster the morale of her troops. But the financial backing essential to the battle had come, as we know, from Abravanel, the Jew, who was now in exile. Not a single believing Jew was left in all of Spain or in the Balearic Islands. The Muslims were defeated. Spain was a purely Catholic country. It was a year of many fulfillments.

And on August 3, 1492, another glorious triumph was beginning. Christopher Columbus sailed his three ships toward an unknown world on a voyage which was to fulfill two of the great goals of Spain, gold and honor. This strange, adventurous man who was considered a charlatan by many, an "eccentric traveller with a flair for histrionic gestures" by others, became the center of attention.

His famous journal begins with a sentence which, rather oddly, connects his expedition with the expulsion of the Jews: "After the Spanish monarchs had expelled all the Jews from their Kingdom and lands in January [he apparently forgot that the edict was issued a few months later, in March] in that same month they commissioned me to undertake the voyage to India with a properly equipped fleet." No other contemporary event has been so connected. The Christian reaction to the expulsion was quite mild, not much fuss was made about it. The mention of it as a major event, a milestone in Spanish history, was left to Columbus, who was so secretive about his origins that Bernáldez thought he "looked and sounded like a person from another land." He was referring to the exotic, outlandish manners which Columbus affected. As a matter of fact, Columbus never called himself by his real name, Cristoforo Colombo, but preferred to call himself Cristóbal Colón.

There has been much speculation that Columbus himself might have been a Marrano. The Spanish historian Salvador de Madariaga is convinced that Columbus was descended from a Jewish family which, after conversion, moved to Italy. He cites a case in which "at the great auto-da-fé at Tarragona, on July 18, 1489, clothed in the garb of penitence, Andreas Colón, his wife Blanca, and his mother-in-law Francisca Colón. . . . all confessed that they had observed rites, ceremonies and holy days of the Jews" and he adds, "What must have been the feelings of Christopher Columbus when he heard that members of the Jewish race bore his name and had been condemned by the Inquisition." It seems to be common knowledge that Colón was an old

Spanish-Jewish family name, but it is less certain that Columbus was a Marrano.

What is known is that Jews, as well as Marranos, played a role in making the expedition possible and participated in the voyage itself. The influential Marrano Luis Santanel was among the few who took the young Columbus seriously, and it was he who arranged the first audience for him at the court. He also advanced seventeen thousand florins to the crown to help finance the voyage. Other Marranos and Jews became involuntary backers of Columbus when fortunes confiscated from them helped defray the cost of the second journey.

The maps that Columbus used were prepared by the Jewish cartographer Abraham Zacuto, and the naval academy which had a part in planning the trip was headed by another Jew, Yehuda Crescas, a famous map maker and son of the philosopher Abraham Crescas.

On board Columbus' ship there were many Marranos. The list that has come down to us includes Rodrigo Sánchez, superintendent; Dr. Marco, ship's surgeon; and Mesta Bernal, the physician. Luis de Torres, a Jew who had been converted just a day before the ship sailed, served as official interpreter, and a Marrano, Rodrigo de Triana, was the seaman who sighted the first land. Most of the crew returned to Spain with Columbus. Only De Torres stayed, and in Cuba he returned to Judaism. He was the first member of the large communities of Judaizing Marranos who went to the New World and were soon to become active in the development of the new export trade.

The fifteenth century ended with Spanish Jewry completely devastated. Thousands had lost their lives. A quarter of a million had been forced into baptism, and many of them lived precariously and unhappily in the twilight zone of Marranic existence, between the Church and a synagogue which no longer existed. The Inquisition had put to death thousands of Judaizing heretics and reduced the remainder to the status of beggars. And at the end of the century the most radical cure for the "incurable disease" of Judaism had been found. The Jews were expelled. The glorious and tragic history of Spanish Jewry had come to an end.

This woeful inventory of Jewish experience amounted to a catalogue of victories for the Spanish church and state. The Church had good reason to feel triumphant. If conversion of the infidels was a Christian goal, it had been fully realized. Not only Jews but also Muslims had found refuge in the Church. These Marranos and Moriscos, who had been discovered sliding back into old habits, had been uncovered by the Inquisition, which the Church considered Christ's own Supreme Court on earth during twenty dark years, illuminated only by the fires of countless autos-da-fé.

Ferdinand and Isabella could look back on their reign with the greatest satisfaction. Until the very end, they had benefited from the invaluable services of their court Jews, their physicians, their tax collectors, financial advisers and skillful statesmen. The expulsion was the greatest coup of all. It had rid the country of the last of the Jews and had filled the empty treasury of the state with millions. The colonial system in the newly discovered territories established Spain as a major maritime power and was bound to bring new wealth to the country.

At the end of the fifteenth century the Marranos were no longer a national problem. The process of integration into Spanish society of the fifty thousand new *conversos* who were a legacy of the expulsion was almost complete. The number of Marranos who never ate pork or who abstained from bread during the week of Passover dwindled considerably. It may have been that it was too risky to indulge in these customs while the Inquisition was in power, but it was probably simply that most of them had forgotten their Jewish heritage. Many had taken their places in the Spanish economy or were holding offices in the Church. Others were integrated into caballero families, and through intermarriage there was hardly a family in the urban population which did not have some Jewish blood. For the first fifty years of the sixteenth century there was no more talk of *conversos*. But one more chapter remained to be written.

With the deaths of Isabella in 1504 and Ferdinand in 1514, the reign of the Hapsburgs began. Charles V and his successor, Philip II, two foreigners, entangled Spain in European affairs after centuries of isolation. Spain went to war with France and England. In 1588 her great Armada was destroyed, and after these adventures Spain found herself depopulated and impoverished despite the gold that came from her overseas possessions. It was in this atmosphere that the *conversos* again moved into the center of Spanish life.

Internal problems and international defeats in battle gave rise to a spirit of chauvinism in sixteenth-century Spain which can be compared to the climate in Germany in the 1930s when that country also grappled with internal economic problems and suffered from a lowering of international prestige. In the face of Spain's deterioration, the Spaniards began to develop a racial theory and practice similar to Hitler's Nuremberg Laws, which declared all races except the Aryan to be impure. In Spain the edict was called the *Estatutes de Limpieza de Sangre*, Statutes of the Purity of Blood. It had been promulgated in 1449 and was used by the Inquisition throughout its reign, but it was not in general use until the sixteenth century because Spain until that time was too successful a nation to have need of such a law. It required a collective sense of inferiority to be generally accepted.

The spirit of the time was expressed in a book on the Spanish nobility which was published in 1533. The author, Juan Acre de Otalore, stated that Spain was the oldest country in the world, and that the very demeanor and physiognomy of the Spanish noblemen were proof of their superiority to any other race in the world. The most outrageous assertions were made seriously. De Otalore proclaimed that Spanish philosophers wrote a thousand years before Plato; that Spaniards were Christians a thousand years before Christ was born; that Tubal, Noah's grandson, had come to Spain at the time of the great flood and that it was the Spanish people, rather than the Jews, who were elected from "all nations of the world." He also listed five characteristics which distinguished Spaniards from any other people. He called these the *cinco excelencias:* military valor, great wealth, pure literary taste, a combination of knowledge and the most devout piety, and genuine nobility. To this was added the most important ingredient: purity of blood.

But since Jewish blood had contaminated the Spanish population, racial purity was obviously lacking and had to be restored. The old forgotten *Estatutes de Limpieza de Sangre* were now unearthed to become the accepted law of the land. And since there were no longer any Jews in the country, the *conversos* and their descendants became the main target.

The new anti-Jewish measures were promulgated and supported by the Cathedral of Toledo, which considered itself the national shrine in Spain, only slightly less important to Catholics than St. Peter's in Rome. The most passionate agitator for racial purity was Juan Martínez Silecese, the Archbishop of the Cathedral of Toledo. Since he came from peasant stock, he was opposed by the clergy of noble descent. In general, the cry for *Limpieza de Sangre* came from the burghers and lower classes. The nobility had good reason for opposing it, since scarcely a noble family could claim racial purity. To permit the promulgation of a law of racial purity meant inviting endless family disgrace. It was easy enough to ascertain that the mothers of important members of noble families had been Marranos and, at times, even accused of Judaizing practices. The lower classes had nothing to fear from a law which required sworn testimony to the racial purity of people in high positions. The nobility was not so calm.

The greatest scandals were created within the Church itself, and particularly in some monastic orders which, as we have seen, had provided sanctuary for many Marranos, both sincere and insincere converts. Ignatius of Loyola had called the statutes an insult to Jesus and his apostles, all of whom had been Jews. But after his death and that of his Marrano successor, only *limpios*, those free of Jewish blood, were permitted to lead the order. Because of the edict the Jesuits lost their social prestige, and the sons of noble families preferred to join the Dominicans, where they were sure to meet caballeros.

The law which had now been generally accepted was not

simple to enforce. At the universities, some of which had enthusiastically voted for racial purity, as well as in the major churches, former Marranos occupied high positions. The literary scene was replete with important writers who did not even attempt to conceal their Jewish origins. There were many cases of high dignitaries who were proven to be of "mixed" royal and Jewish blood. Perhaps because of their importance, it was decided that these Marranos who held high positions would not be eliminated, but none of them would be promoted.

Withholding information of racial impurity was punishable by heavy fines. In order to prove the racial purity of a family, two witnesses were required, and it is easy to imagine how corrupt the procedure of "proving" the proper lineage became. Bribes were commonplace. Documents were destroyed and new ones manufactured. Forgery and lies were the order of the day. As in the days of the Inquisition, one could trust neither servants nor the members of one's own families. Thousands of people, no longer conscious of their Marrano descent, were discovered and accused of being "impure." Informers prospered.

Contemporary foreign observers shook their heads in disbelief at this new Spanish chauvinism. One of them wrote:

Spain is not the only country in Europe which has experienced the presence of Jews, Muslims and other infidels. But in France where Jews were confronted with the choice of conversion or expulsion under three kings, those who preferred to remain in France and convert were simply known as Christians and were not molested by a statute of racial impurity, nor by the appellation "Jew" or "New Christian." When a Frenchman visits Spain, it is assumed that he is an Old Christian, but when a Spaniard visits France he is known to be a Marrano. What else would prompt him to leave his own country?

A Spanish cleric, Padre Pedro, was even more critical:

If it were true that Jewish blood is identical with evil character, how are we to account for the numerous and remarkable examples of true piety and devotion on the part of men of Jewish blood? We Spaniards have finally succeeded in creating a nation of madmen. We still distinguish between New and Old Christians, while other countries which permit their Jews to pray in their synagogues do not seem to feel menaced by Judaism. It is a shame that our country, mentally sick as it is, searches for Jewish blood which hardly exists, almost a hundred years after the expulsion of the Jews. With such an attitude it can only bring dishonor on itself.

Whenever birth or antecedents determine the social status and the acceptance of a people, there is no escape. The promulgation of the racial laws and the continued existence of the Inquisition made life for the Marranos in Spain intolerable. The only solution was emigration. In spite of strict laws prohibiting Marranos or their offspring from leaving the country, thousands of ships, often piloted by bribed captains, left the harbors of Spain bearing the New Christians from their homes in Spain and Portugal to the many countries which were willing to accept them. Soon there were Marranos in many parts of Europe. Others went to the new territories of the recently discovered Indies: the Caribbean islands, Brazil, Peru and Mexico.

The integration of the Marranos into the social and economic structure of their new homelands was incredibly rapid. The ready welcome they received must not be supposed to have been based on altruism on the part of the governments of these countries. It was founded on the simple notion that *"pecunia no olet."* The new immigrants brought with them large fortunes, and capital from the hands of Jews was as useful as that from the hands of Gentiles. So the Marrano dispersion had the effect of permitting Jewish immigrants to participate in the development of the new capitalism. Others contributed their talents, intelligence and energies to the natural sciences, philosophy and medicine which were developing almost as fast as the new commerce.

Among the Spanish Marranos only the rich and educated were able to pay the ransom for their emigration. The poor remained in the "old country." They were at last completely integrated into the population and were soon forgotten. But of the Marranos who emigrated, there is much to remember. In the history of emigration, their story forms a unique chapter of achievement.

Chapter Three

Some of the seventeenth-century Marrano emigrants from Spain and Portugal went to Muslim countries. But the majority immigrated to the Papal States of Italy and to other Christian lands, and a particularly large and creative Jewish community was established by Marranos in the Netherlands, where Amsterdam became the center of that country's Jewish population. Because the early days of this settlement were recorded as a "Memorial for the Coming Generations" by the community's first rabbi, we have a good idea of what life was like for this group of immigrants. Those who went to other countries undoubtedly had similar experiences.

What was to become one of the cultural centers of Sephardic Judaism began modestly. As Rabbi Uri Halevi tells it, he was living in the seaport of Emden in the year 1604, when ten Spanish Marranos and four boys with all their "wares, furniture and household goods which constituted a large fortune" arrived in two small boats. Above the door of the rabbi's house was a Hebrew inscription, but the Spanish immigrants who walked by on a tour of the city could not read Hebrew. They did, however, notice that a goose was just being delivered. This inspired them to return to their inn and ask the innkeeper to buy them a goose for their dinner. The innkeeper happened to buy the goose from the rabbi. When he reported to the strangers that he had bought their dinner from "the Jew," they were astonished and pleased to have found one of their people, and the next day, following the innkeeper's direction, they returned to the house with the Hebrew inscription over the door and introduced themselves as Marranos. They said they wanted to have themselves circumcised so that they could return to the religion of their ancestors, and they asked the rabbi to help them establish a Jewish community.

Since Emden was a Lutheran stronghold, the rabbi discouraged them from settling there, suggesting instead that they travel to Amsterdam, rent a house on Junkerstraat across from the Montalbaan Tower, and wait for him to arrive within the month. This they did. At the appointed time the rabbi appeared in Amsterdam, and all ten men and four boys were circumcised, and a room in the house was set aside for services.

Yet not all of Amsterdam was hospitable to the new settlers. Some Flemish citizens complained to the mayor about the "people from Spain who had themselves circumcised by two out-of-town Jews and had set aside a room for daily prayers." The rabbi and his son were ordered to be put under arrest. With some difficulty they persuaded the authorities that the wealthy new immigrants would be an asset to the city, and that if they were allowed to establish their Jewish community there, other equally prosperous settlers would soon follow. Eventually, permission was granted for the Jews to settle in Amsterdam "with every freedom in the world. . . . to live in accordance with Jewish law and religion and to build a house of worship." The rabbi from Emden became the spiritual leader of the community, and his son became its cantor.

It was not long until the news of the freedom granted to the Jews of Amsterdam spread to Spain and Portugal, and many other Marrano families arrived to take up residence there. The rabbi circumcised the newly arrived men and boys, instructing the immigrants in the precepts of Judaism, and he wrote the rules and bylaws of what became the Holy Jewish Community of Amsterdam.

The Marranos who immigrated to Amsterdam found the Dutch to be a sober, industrious and rather adventurous people, citizens of a nation involved in world affairs, prominent in international trade and tolerant—as we have seen—toward anyone who could contribute to this new, open and very commercial community. The Netherlands had gained its independence from Spain in 1581, but even prior to that date it had rapidly conquered the world trade market. Through their control of the East and West India trading companies, the Dutch were among the most prominent and successful traders in the world.

Thanks to the painters of that time, we have a graphic idea of the seventeenth-century Hollander's life, and we know how he looked. The Breughels depicted the world of the burgher and farmer; Frans Hals painted portraits that conveyed the Dutchman's zest for life; Ruisdael made the heavy skies over the dull Dutch landscape look dramatic; and most important, Rembrandt broke through the conventional portrait art of his predecessors and discovered the landscape of the human face, which he painted without flattery to his subjects. Rembrandt considered the new

Jewish immigrants as the authentic descendants of the great Biblical figures, and he often used Jews as models for his remarkable interpretations of the Old and New Testaments. Amsterdam had become a Protestant bulwark and, through French Huguenot immigration, largely Calvinistic. The Calvinist creed which held that prosperity in this world was an indication of God's favor, fitted admirably into the enterprising spirit of the time, and so did the new Marrano immigrants. In this economic, political and cultural climate they developed their own life. Soon they were an autonomous community with a neighborhood of their own—the Jodenbreestraat—where Portuguese and Spanish, rather than the language of the land, were spoken. Most of the books of the Marrano scholars and writers continued to be written in their mother tongues or in Latin. (Other communities created their own Judeo-Spanish known as Ladino, just as the German Jews who found refuge in Eastern Europe had created Yiddish from medieval German.) There was evidently no insistence on linguistic assimilation by the Dutch authorities as long as the Jewish settlers remained law-abiding, productive citizens. And this they seem to have been.

The growth of the Jewish community was phenomenal. New Christians, eager to return to Judaism, seemed to come from everywhere. The promise of religious freedom, coupled with material success, attracted not only those who came directly from the Iberian Peninsula, but others who had already established themselves in North Africa, Italy and Turkey. Soon Amsterdam was known as the "New Jerusalem." In addition to those Marranos who came to declare themselves as Jews, there were some Spanish and

Portuguese Christians, notably in the diplomatic community, who revealed their Jewish origins and became active in the numerous Jewish communal activities. Approximately a hundred Jewish organizations came into being, and in Amsterdam alone, the number of Marranos who returned to Judaism had risen to four thousand by the middle of the seventeenth century.

They established a Jewish school system whose curriculum was so thorough and disciplined that it challenges any of the Jewish schools of today. They erected synagogues. Today's visitor to Amsterdam can still admire the Sephardic synagogue built in 1675. The magnificent mahogany ark was built with wood sent to Amsterdam by Marranos who had settled in Pernambuco, one of the many Marrano communities in Brazil. There were two additional houses of worship and both were luxuriously decorated to reflect the prosperity of the congregations. It is reported that a wedding held in one of these, in the seventeenth century, was attended by guests whose combined wealth was estimated at forty million florins.

But in spite of this growth and prosperity, for many of the Marrano immigrants of the seventeenth century the return to Judaism had created doubts and conflicts. It was, of course, not their exile that made them unique; Jews have always been immigrants. Throughout their history they were forced to leave countries which had been their homelands for centuries. Often they had to find new homes not in the country of their choice, but in any land that would accept them. They had to make difficult economic and linguistic adjustments, but slowly they rebuilt their lives. And however desperate their poverty, however rigorous their new life, the Jews usually managed to transfer their heritage virtually intact to the new world, wherever it was. The self-contained little societies they founded provided them with sustenance and security. It may not have been home, but to the new immigrant it looked very much like home. His wife cooked the familiar old-world specialties; in time there was probably a replica of the little synagogue he had left behind, and the new congregation was, more often than not, made up of friends and relatives who had emigrated with him. The things that had formed his spiritual life in the past had not changed much. Whatever difficulties he experienced in the outside world, on his own ethnic island the immigrant was safe. His poverty may have been appalling, but he found compensation in the rich heritage which had always been central to his life.

This was not true of the Marranos who left Spain and Portugal in the sixteenth and seventeenth centuries. Though in their case the adjustment to the outside world may have been easier because they did not have to contend with poverty, in regard to their Jewishness they were virtually bankrupt. They had declared that they wanted to live as Jews, but they had no heritage to transfer to the new world; they had forsaken their homes, but they had left no little *shul* or synagogue behind. They had, at best, only a very limited notion, a distorted memory, of what it meant to be Jewish. For three generations they had been Catholics without faith, and now they were Jews without knowledge. The religion to which they were so eager to return was, in reality, quite foreign to them.

There had been waves of Marranic immigration dating back to 1492, and the character of each of these exiles was different. The Marranos who left Spain and Portugal in the fifteenth century, perhaps only a decade after conversion to Christianity, had experienced Jewish life, knew Hebrew and were, on the whole, quite knowledgeable about Jewish laws and observance. So if the seventeenth-century immigrants were ignorant of Jewish customs and practices, the Sephardic centers to which they came afforded them ample opportunity for a religious re-education. In each of them they found a knowledgeable Jew, like the rabbi of Emden, who instructed them in Jewish law. But often, and especially for the intellectuals among them, the facts of Jewish life were quite different from what they had expected.

Traditionally, the Jews of Spain had practiced a Judaism that was much freer, more flexible, than that observed by the Ashkenazic Jews of Eastern Europe. The religion of the Sephardim in exile, however, was unbendingly restrictive and intolerant of any deviation from Orthodox practice. Having recently returned from what they considered to have been Christian idolatry, the Sephardim, no doubt, felt that they had to prove good faith again and again. Obedience to the strictest rules was a prerequisite of Jewish survival for a people who had been professing—and often believing— Catholics. Even some of the outstanding Sephardic rabbis were not more than one generation removed from Christianity. So they were very conscious of the Orthodox establishment of the Eastern ghetto and felt that they were under the scrutiny of the rabbis of Brest Litovsk, Vilna and other Ashkenazic centers; these rabbis were, after all, not "returnees" to Judaism and were therefore considered representatives of authoritative, authentic faith. So while the Sephardim added some Spanish embellishments to the traditional rituals, they took their cues from the Orthodox rabbis of the East and often consulted them on questions of religious practice.

The overwhelming majority of the seventeenth-century

immigrants, accustomed to Catholic authoritarianism, well-defined doctrines and enforced theological discipline, probably found nothing objectionable in an equally compulsive Judaism. The flight from rigid Catholicism to Jewish restrictiveness must have seemed quite natural to them. Some Sephardic customs even contained faint echoes of Catholic rituals. To this day, for instance, the Sephardi throws a kiss at the Holy Ark as he enters the synagogue, gesturing with a reverence similar to that of the Catholic who kneels and crosses himself as he approaches the altar of his church. On the whole, then, the "returning" Marranos felt quite at home in the Sephardic synagogue with its solemnity and its churchlike formality. Most of them also found security in the six hundred and thirteen commandments and prohibitions which were the backbone of Orthodox Jewish existence.

But there was an important minority which had doubts. Some simply had difficulty in understanding the Jewish precepts and the kind of Judaism which had developed during the decades of their family's Catholic existence. Others suffered from a more complicated religious dilemma which was, in part, a reflection of the time in which they lived.

The seventeenth century was an era of doubt and conflict. At the center of religious life there were three clearly defined orbits of faith: the Catholic Church, freshly invigorated by the Counter Reformation which met the challenge of Martin Luther with new fervor and increased emphasis on the Church doctrines; the new religious phenomenon of Protestantism in its various forms, including groups similar to the Calvinists who were very active in the new capitalist era, but as stubborn in their beliefs as the

Catholics; and the Jews, not very many in number, but bent on preserving the ancient traditions, a task in which they were assisted by the isolation of the ghetto. These three worlds were firmly established. Their adherents found security in their respective faith world: the Christians in sin and salvation, the Jews in law and justice. All three were in clear conflict with the new intellectual world of the times and with its newly born skepticism.

While the vast majority of the world's population still held fast to its religious convictions, the intellectuals of Venice, Florence, Paris and Amsterdam began to have doubts about the blind acceptance of religious dogma. Science began to replace God. The new man of the seventeenth century lived in the sphere of *sic et non* ("yes as well as no") upon which Pierre Abélard had speculated in the twelfth century. Some of the intellectuals among the Marranos had come in contact with this new, questioning world, and their personal Jewish problem was, to a large extent, a similar conflict. They were also faced with a "yes and no" choice. They were no-longer Christians, but not-yet Jews. Their inability to come to terms with this problem brought them into discord with existing Jewish communities and into sharp differences with the rabbinical world, which could not tolerate them.

In 1660 Isaac Orobio de Castro, himself a Marrano and therefore abler than most to analyze the Jewish-Marrano conflict, described the situation in Amsterdam. What he observed is applicable to other cities in which Marranos lived. De Castro first praises these Marranos "who have left the idolatry [of Spain and Portugal], who undergo circumcision as soon as they arrive, love God's law and are eager to learn that which they and their ancestors had forgotten during the years of their imprisonment." He admires their humility and their eagerness to listen to those who are knowledgeable and able to explain the meaning of Judaism of which they know so little. But for some of the Marranos he has only a severe admonition:

> There is another group that returns to Judaism who indulges in the idolatries of logic, metaphysics and medicine. They are not less ignorant about the Divine Law than the others, but they are full of vanity, haughtiness and a sense of superiority because they believe they know everything although, of course, they know not the most essential. They place themselves under the happy yoke of Judaism and begin to listen to our explanations. But their vanity and so-called superiority prevents them from accepting our teachings. They use sophistic arguments against everything that is sacred and divine, only for the purpose of appearing to be witty, scientific and intellectually keen. The trouble is, that the young and the ignorant admire them and follow suit. They all land quickly in the abyss of atheism and apostasy.

Neither the Sephardic nor the Ashkenazic rabbinical authorities displayed patience with these apostates. They called for their excommunication. The Ashkenazim, who were consulted in such cases, judged these troubled "New Jews" with customary rigidity, leaving no room for a consideration of the psychological problems of a Jewish convert who had lived under the Cross for many generations and had come in contact with the new Renaissance world dominating the intellectuals of that time. (Among these "deviates," for example, were several physicians who viewed Jewish customs and beliefs as medieval, since they had been trained in the new natural sciences, which often conflicted with Jewish doctrines.) The Sephardic rabbis, some of whom had lived under the Inquisition or had lost relatives to the autos-da-fé, were even more severe. It is understandable that they had to watch over the purity of their new faith, but they lacked the compassion which might have helped greatly in overcoming the conflicts of conscience and conviction which plagued so many of the Marranos. As survivors of the Inquisition, the rabbis could have been expected to practice understanding and forgiveness. Instead, they created their own Jewish form of Inquisition, replete with informers, and although they did not kill the transgressors, they demolished their lives through the pronouncement of the *herem*, the official excommunication.

In contrast to their harsh attitudes toward those who deviated from strict Orthodox interpretations of the Jewish law, the rabbinical community was rather liberal when it came to accepting "returning" Marranos. We know of no case of rejection of any of those who wanted to return to Judaism, even though they had lived "in sin" for generations, unable and often unwilling to commemorate the highest Jewish holidays, the dietary laws and many other Jewish rituals. "An Israelite, although he had sinned, is still an Israelite," the rabbis said in an astonishingly generous interpretation. All the Christian practices, the prayers in the Church, the Hail Marys and Pater Nosters, were wiped out in that one sentence, as were the infractions of the dietary laws and other sins against the Jewish faith. A Marrano who expressed a readiness to return from his "Babylonian exile" was accepted without question. But once he returned to Judaism, the strict law applied to him. Any deviation from Jewish belief received the harshest of penalties, solemn public excommunication from the community.

Uriel da Costa and Baruch Spinoza are the two outstanding cases of public excommunication from the great Marrano community of Amsterdam. Their lives and their fate present us with two extreme examples of what it meant to be a secret Jew who returned to his people. Although an artist of the nineteenth century painted Da Costa as a grown man playing with a child who was supposed to be Spinoza, the two probably never met. They are shown together, no doubt, because their common fate has linked them in history, though we remember Da Costa only because of his excommunication.

Uriel da Costa was born in Portugal in 1585 into a family that had converted to Christianity in the fifteenth century. From 1604 to 1608 he was a student at the Collegium Coimbrese, a college of the Jesuit University of Coimbra, where he studied canonical law. He received the first consecration of a priest as a young man of twenty-five and was elected treasurer of the main church in his hometown of Oporto. Five years later he fled to Amsterdam with his mother, Sarah, and his four brothers, Aaron, Mordecai, Abraham and Joseph. What prompted him to leave his homeland so that he could return to the religion of his Jewish forefathers is best described by Da Costa himself in the moving autobiography he called *Exemplar Humanae Vitae* ("Example of a Human Life"). This is the beginning of that remarkable document:

I was born in Portugal in the city which bears the name of the country and which is usually called Oporto. My parents were members of the nobility. They were descendants of those Jews who were once upon a time in this very country forced to embrace the Christian religion. My father was a believing Christian, but a man of strict honor who emphasized his rank and station in life. It was in this house that I grew up in accordance with his status. We never lacked for servants, neither did we lack for noble Spanish horses in our stables which we used for horseback riding. My father was a master at it, and I followed his example early in life. After undergoing training in many fields in accordance with tradition among people of our standing, I decided to devote myself to jurisprudence. . . . It is unbelievable what I had to suffer because of religion. According to the tradition of the country I grew up in the Roman Catholic religion, and since I was terribly afraid of eternal damnation, I was very eager to observe the tradition punctiliously. I occupied myself with the reading of the New Testament and other spiritual books, read the summation of the Defenders of the Faith, and the more I thought of them the greater were the difficulties I experienced. Finally, I became completely confused. I was consumed by fear and anxiety, by sorrow and pain. It seemed to me impossible to confess the sins in accordance with Roman Catholic custom so as to obtain proper absolution, and I found it impossible to fulfill what was demanded. I was desperate thinking of the redemption of the soul, as it was indeed true that it could only be achieved by following the rules of the Roman Church. But because I found it difficult to give up a religion to which I was accustomed since birth and which had deeply affected me in my faith, I began to doubt at the age of twenty-two whether it was really true what I was taught of the life to come. I tried to reconcile faith with reason, for it was reason which whispered into my ear something utterly irreconcilable with faith. . . .

Since I could not find any peace within the Roman Catholic religion, and since I was longing to find some satisfaction in any religion, I began to read the Books of Moses and the Prophets, knowing full well that there was great competition between Jew and Christian. In the Old Testament I found many things which contradicted the New Testament completely, and what was said of God there offered fewer difficulties. In addition to this, the old covenant is accepted by

Jews as well as Christians, and the new one only by Christians. Finally I began to believe in Moses and decided to live according to his law because he received it from God, or so he maintained, and he simply considered himself an intermediary called to his office by God himself or even forced into it.

Considering all this and taking into consideration the fact that in the country in which I lived there was no freedom of religion, I decided to change my residence and to leave the home in which I and my fathers had lived. I did not think twice about giving up my ecclesiastical office and relinquishing it to somebody else. I did not think of either my advantage or my reputation which were in jeopardy at that time. I left my beautiful house situated in the best neighborhood of the city, a house which was built by my father. So we embarked on a ship under the greatest danger, for it is known that those descended from Jews were not permitted to leave the country without a particular permit by the king. My mother was with me, as well as my brothers, whom I had won over to my newly won convictions about religion. It was a daring enterprise which could have failed, so dangerous was it in this country to even discuss matters of religion. It was a long voyage, and we finally arrived in Amsterdam, where we felt the Jews could live in freedom and fulfill the commandments. And since I was imbued with it, my brothers and I immediately submitted to circumcision.

After the first few days I began to understand that the customs and institutions of the Jews were not at all in accordance with what Moses had written. If Moses' commandments had to be observed strictly as written, then the Jews were wrong to have invented so many things which deviated from the laws of Moses. I believed in doing something pleasing to God if I defended freely and openly the law of Moses. The present-day sages of the Jews have maintained both their customs and their evil character. They still fight stubbornly for the sect and the institution of the despicable Pharisees not entirely unselfishly, for it is true what many people have said, that they do all these things in order to sit in the first row of the temple and to be greeted in the market place with particular respect. They would not permit me to deviate from their opinion in the slightest, but indicated to me that it was my duty to accept every little bit of their interpretation. If I would not do so, they said, they would have to threaten me with exclusion from the community, and indeed with complete excommunication, both in terms of theology and human relations. I believe it was not right for a man who had exchanged security at home for freedom abroad, and who had sacrificed every possible advantage to permit himself to be so threatened. I believe that in the light of such circumstances it was neither right nor fair nor manly to submit to people who were not even permitted to sit in judgment in a court. So I decided to take everything upon myself and insist upon my opinion. This is the reason why I was excommunicated by the community. Even my brothers, whose teacher I was, passed me by, so afraid were they of the authorities that they did not even greet me on the street.

Like many of their contemporaries, Da Costa's family knew only that they were New Christians, Christians of Jewish descent. But "my father was a believing Christian," Da Costa tells us. And so was he himself until he began to doubt the validity of Christian theology. His concept of Judaism was based on his reading of the Old Testament, which he found more acceptable than the New Testament. So when he left Portugal for Amsterdam in search of his ancestors' faith, he had expected to find a Biblical Judaism which, of course, no longer existed.

There have been several fundamentalist Jewish sects which insisted that Judaism be based on Biblical writings and the observance only of Biblical commandments. At the time of Jesus the aristocratic Sadducees insisted on this kind of adherence to the written law; in the early Middle Ages the Karaites lived in accordance with the commandments of the Torah and rejected any new interpretation of what they considered divine law. Da Costa was a throwback to the Sadducees and the Karaites. Soon after his arrival in Amsterdam he realized that the Judaism of the Sephardim and Ashkenazim had little in common with the Biblical ideal for which he was searching. In the course of the centuries, Judaism has become interpreted law. It had become a rabbinical faith built upon the authoritative interpretations of the written law by the rabbi who insisted that even such a well-known commandment as "Thou shalt keep the Sabbath" could not be understood without the rabbinical commentary which defined the observance of the holy day.

It was the historical reality of Judaism that Da Costa and many of his fellow Marranos found hard to accept. Since they had not been part of the historic development of their faith, they depended on the Bible for their information about it. The rabbi is not mentioned in the Old Testament, and in Da Costa's reading of the New Testament he had apparently overlooked the new rabbinical Judaism which was personified by Rabbi Jesus of Nazareth, who fought against the Pharisees.

Samuel da Silva—the physician and Jewish scholar who had attended Da Costa's circumcision, taught him Judaism and introduced him to the synagogue—did not have any insight into this serious, yet naïve young man and did not make him understand the realities of contemporary Jewish practice. Later Da Silva even wrote an angry thesis against his former pupil.

There was something masochistic about Da Costa, and

although one is often deeply touched by the calamities to which he was subjected, one sometimes suspects him of having actually enjoyed them. This may be a harsh judgment; yet his refusal to learn and accept the reality of Jewish life (even without identifying it) is astounding. It speaks not merely of stubbornness, but perhaps also of a lack of simple intelligence. Spinoza, who had deeper doubts about Judaism, drew the consequences: he disapproved and left it. Da Costa wanted to change two thousand years of history. Even the most naïve should have anticipated fierce resistance on the part of the religious establishment. The result was a tortured, frustrated, desperate life and an even more hopeless end.

In addition to his autobiography, two of Da Costa's writings have survived, each of which caused an immediate contemporary response. His "Theses Against Tradition" (*Propostas contra a tradição*) and "On the Immortality of the Human Soul" (*Sobre a mortalidade de alma do homen*) both touched and wounded the fundamental concerns of Orthodox Judaism. In both books his source is the Bible. Nowhere in the Bible, he claims, does he find justification for most of the practiced Jewish customs, nor does the Bible speak of resurrection or immortality of the soul. His two contentions are correct, but the customs had grown out of the daily life of the Jews of which Da Costa knew nothing.

The "Theses Against Tradition" was written while Da Costa was on a mission attending to the family's banking business in Hamburg. He forwarded some of his first anti-rabbinical theses, dealing with phylacteries, circumcision, dietary laws and other Jewish customs, through one of the bank's messengers to León da Modena, the chief rabbi of Venice, one of the richest and most influential Jewish communities. No doubt the bank negotiated many business transactions in that city and was in communication with fellow Marranos in the banking business. The response was immediate and negative. The chief rabbi of Venice refuted all of his arguments. Neither Da Costa nor the Jews of Venice knew how many doubts had beset Da Modena's soul. He had written a passionate book against gambling, one of the pastimes of the people of Venice in which the Jews lustily participated. After his death he was discovered to have been a very active gambler himself, with considerable gambling debts which had to be paid by the community. However, during his lifetime he was respected as a great Sephardic rabbinical authority. He recommended Da Costa's excommunication to the rabbis of Hamburg, and since Da Costa had already left for the Netherlands he was excommunicated *in absentia* in Venice. In Amsterdam, where he wrote his tractate against the immortality of the soul, he did not fare much better:

A boy, actually the son of my sister who lived with me, went to the community leaders and accused me of eating food which was not in accordance with Jewish law, and said that I could not possibly be a Jew. It is because of this denunciation that a new war against me ensued. That cousin who [had previously] intervened on my behalf . . . claimed this could be interpreted to my disadvantage, and since he was very proud and pretentious, in addition to being ignorant and impudent, he began an open war against me, causing all my brothers to side with him. . . . In addition to this domestic war, a public war ensued which was carried on by the rabbis and the people. They began to persecute me with a new hatred and did so many things against me that I could only react with utter and justified contempt.

In the meantime something new happened. By chance I had a conversation with two people who came from London to Amsterdam, one an Italian and the other a Spaniard. They were Christians and not of Jewish descent. After I explained my situation to them, they asked my advice about admission into the Jewish community and conversion to the Jewish religion. I advised them against both, telling them to remain what they were, as they did not know what kind of yoke they were about to be burdened with. However, I asked them not to mention our conversation to the Jews, and they promised they would not. But these scoundrels betrayed me, thinking of nothing but their own gain, which they hoped they would receive as a token of gratitude from my dear friends, the Pharisees. As soon as they learned about my conversation, the elders of the synagogue met with the rabbis, who were hot with anger. The mob that had assembled there during the meeting cried out: "Crucify him! Crucify him!" I was invited to appear before the Great Council. There I was told with great solemnity, as though we were talking about a matter of life and death, that if I was a Jew I should await their judgment and act accordingly. If I was not a Jew, they would again excommunicate me. . . . Then they read from a document in which it was written that I had to appear in the synagogue wearing garments of mourning and holding a black candle in my hand, repeating certain horrible words in public assembly that my action was depicted as outrageous and sacrilegious. I then was supposed to be publicly whipped with a leather whip, after to lie down over the threshold of the synagogue so that everyone assembled there could walk across my body. In addition, I was held to fast on certain days. Upon reading this document I was boiling inside, and an unquenchable anger seized me. However, I controlled myself and simply replied that I could not possibly be expected to do all this. After hearing me out they decided to again excommunicate me from the Jewish community. Some were evidently not satisfied with such judgment and spat at me when they saw me in the street, among them being children who had learned such behavior from their parents.

We do not know the exact number of excommunications imposed on Da Costa. It may be that he was also excommunicated by some of the Ashkenazic East European communities. It is unthinkable that the Ashkenazim would have been silent about Da Costa when even Venice demanded the ban.

The ceremony itself was painful. It did not reconcile Da Costa. Had he been more courageous, or at least wiser, he would have severed his relationship with the Jews altogether. But this he did not do. In spite of the excommunication he returned to his splendid home and persisted in a battle which seems as childish as Don Quixote's attacks on the windmills. He lived in material prosperity and independence, but in incredible loneliness and self-torture. His wife, Sarah, had died but he found it impossible to remarry. After the final excommunication his brothers shunned him altogether. A faithful housekeeper was his only companion. There were no visitors. He lived that way, in dismal wretchedness and misery, for seven years. Finally, although he had not come to any salvation for himself, he decided to ask for reconciliation. He apparently did not realize how deeply denigrating the ceremony of reconciliation would be. He describes it in one of the most moving chapters of his *Exemplar Humanae Vitae:*

I entered the synagogue, which was crowded with men and women who had come to observe this spectacle. When the time came I went to the pulpit from which the rabbi used to preach, and I read in a loud voice the list of my confessions:

"I merit to die a thousand deaths for what I have committed, to wit: desecration of the Sabbath, betrayal of the faith which I insulted to such an extent that I prevented others from converting to Judaism." In order to repent for my sins I would submit to whatever they decide about me and carry every burden laid upon me. I also promised that I would never again repeat all the treacherous acts I had committed. After reading the confession I descended from the altar and the president of the community approached me, whispering in my ear that I was to stand in any of the corners of the synagogue. Going to one of the corners, the sexton approached me and asked me to strip off my clothes. I disrobed to my waist, wrapped a scarf around my head, took off my shoes, and stretched out my arms so that they touched one of the columns of the synagogue. The sexton then tied my hands with ropes to the column. The cantor came, and with a leather whip he was given, beat me 39 times according to the law which provides for 40 lashes. But these people are so conscientious they are afraid they might give me more than the law states. While he whipped me I recited the psalm. When this was over I sat down on the floor and the rabbi came, releasing me from the ban of excommunication as though at this moment the gates of heaven had opened up for me which hitherto had been locked. Then I dressed, and lay down again over the threshold of the synagogue while the sexton held my head. Following this, all the people, men and women, walked over me and out into the street. There were children among them, and also old people. No monkey could have invented a more despicable, tasteless and ridiculous action. Afterward when everybody had left I rose and someone helped me get the dust off my clothes, so that no one should say that I was not treated honorably. Although they had whipped me just a short time ago, they expressed their pity for me and patted my head, and I went home.

The autobiography ends with this passage:

This then is the true story of my life. This is the role I played in this vain theater called the world, in my own vain and restive life. Now I expect to be charged justly by people, justly and without passion, and in the kind of freedom which calls for truth. For this is what behooves men who are men of truth. If you find in my story something which awakens your pity, then you should recognize and bemoan that sad lot of man, for you are part of it.

So that everything is said and nothing is omitted, the name which I bore in Portugal while I was yet a Christian was Gabriel da Costa. When I came to the Jews—I should never have come to them—I changed my name slightly. Today I am called Uriel.

In spite of his reconciliation with the Jewish establishment, Da Costa could not truthfully return to his family, his banking business and the Marrano community as though nothing had happened. He would never forget the humiliation of the ceremony in the synagogue, nor would those who had trampled over him, nor the man who had administered the thirty-nine lashes. So Da Costa saw no way out. Sometime during his seven years of despair Da Costa had bought a pistol. Now he used it to end his life.

In the cemetery in Oudekerk which the Marranos had acquired in 1614 there are many Da Costas, but Uriel's grave is not among them. Because Da Costa was a suicide he was probably interred in an unmarked grave. As he had planned, the *Exemplar Humanae Vitae* became his last will and testament. Reading it now, three hundred years later, we are still moved. It is a bitter document, a story of human woe and vanity, misery, sorrow, stubbornness and frustration. But it is also an example of a very special human life whose form was dictated by the conflict of being a "New Christian" and a secret Jew.

Baruch Spinoza was only eight years old in 1640 when these events took place. He may have been one of the many children at Da Costa's ceremony of reconciliation. He may even have been one of those who walked over his body as he lay prostrate on the threshold. No one knows. Just sixteen years later, the same solemn *herem*, excommunication, was pronounced on Spinoza, banishing him from the Jewish community of Amsterdam just as it had excluded Da Costa. But here the parallel between the two men ends. Spinoza's response to his excommunication was as different from Da Costa's as the two men themselves were different. Once he was excommunicated, Spinoza, the great philosopher, developed his rich intellectual life in complete isolation from the Jewish community which had banned him. Da Costa, who had given up everything to become a Jew, could not live with his exclusion. They were both victims of the same narrow-mindedness, but neither in their lives nor in their temperaments were they at all similar.

The ban against Spinoza was announced on July 27, 1656, in the hearing of the assembled congregation of the community of Amsterdam. It was preceded by a short introduction:

"The leaders of the Jewish community herewith inform you that for a long time they have had knowledge of the evil opinions and actions of Baruch de Espinoza. Through various means and promises we have endeavored to persuade him to leave his evil paths. We could not see any improvement in his terrible heretic thoughts which he lived and taught, and horrendous actions which he committed, about which we received information every day from many trustworthy witnesses. The statements of the witnesses were made in the presence of the aforesaid Espinoza. As all this was done in the presence of our rabbis, who confirmed that these statements had been made, we decided with rabbinical approval that the aforementioned Spinoza be banned and removed from the household of Israel as we now and herewith place the following ban on him:

"In accordance with the decisions of the angels and the judgment of the saints, we ban, expel, and curse Baruch de Espinoza, with the approval of the holy God and this entire congregation. This is done in the presence of our sacred Books of the Law containing the 613 commandments and prohibitions. We ban him with the same ban which was pronounced by Joshua over the city of Jericho, and with the same curses which the Prophet Elishah pronounced over the young man, and with all the curses which are inscribed in the Law. Cursed be he during the day and cursed be he during the night. Cursed be he when he lies down and cursed be he when he returns. God will never pardon him. The anger and wrath of God will always descend on this man and bring all the curses which are written in the Book of the Law. God will destroy his name under the heaven and for evil will he eliminate him from all the tribes of Israel, with all the curses of heaven which are written in the Book of the Law. And you who adhere to the Lord your God will live today and forever.

"We herewith decree that nobody is permitted to communicate with him either directly or in writing, that nobody may do him any favors and that nobody may be permitted to dwell with him under the same roof or approach him within four cubits. Nobody is permitted to read any of his writings published or written by him."

Spinoza was not in the synagogue when the ban was read, nor did he attempt a reconciliation with the congregation.

For some time he had had nothing in common with the community. He was no longer tied by nostalgia, sentiment or loyalty to this group of people whose beliefs he no longer shared. His Hebrew name, Baruch, means "blessed." Now he simply took its Latin equivalent: Benedict. Clearly he did not consider the excommunication as a sign that he was no longer favored by God.

Very few portraits of Spinoza have survived. The most revealing would have been the self-portrait he is known to have painted but which, along with his other drawings and paintings, has been lost. According to Johannes Colerus, one of his biographers, Spinoza was of "medium size, a man with finely cut features. It was easy to see that he was a Portuguese Jew. . . . the color of his skin was swarthy, his hair was long and his eyebrows black." But although Spinoza looked like a Jew and was by birth and training a Sephardi, in this respect as in others his thinking did not fit into the rigid mold demanded by the leaders of the Marrano community. How, then, did this young man of twenty-four come to be accused both of "terrible heretic thoughts" and "horrendous actions"?

Baruch Spinoza was born in Amsterdam into a Jewish family, but he was a Marrano. The family had fled Spain and journeyed to Portugal and France. We do not know how many of them practiced Judaism illegally, but we do know that they arrived in Amsterdam at the beginning of the seventeenth century and were converted according to the law of Moses. The immigrants left many members of the family behind in Spain and Portugal. Eight of them were later incarcerated by the Inquisition for practicing Jewish customs. However, another relative, Don Diego de Espinoza, was made a Grand Inquisitor in spite of his Jewish ancestry. The family's first home was in the Jodenbuurt, near the river Amstel. They later moved to another house, near the Hourgracht, not far from Neveh Shalom, the Portuguese synagogue, where both Abraham Spinoza, Baruch's grandfather, and Michael, his father, held honorary positions. Abraham was the administrator of the Jewish cemetery (where all the Spinozas except Baruch are buried), and Michael was the chairman of the Monte de Piedad, a free-loan society for poor Marranos. Michael did fairly well in his business, and the Spinozas lived comfortably.

The atmosphere in the house was Marranic. The language was Portuguese. The dishes which were served had nothing in common with the cuisine of the Netherlands. There were constant arrivals from "home," and the problems of adjustment to the new country and to the Jewish laws and customs were discussed around the table.

The family also had terrible personal problems. When Baruch was only six, his mother died. She had been his father's second wife. Twice married, he was twice widowed. Of six children, only Baruch and his half-sister Rebecca survived. But personal tragedy was accepted as the natural lot of the Marranos, who had lived with tragedy for so long. The daily stories reported in great detail about the trials, the autos-de-fé and the martyrdom of relatives and friends. Jacob Freudenthal, the nineteenth-century philosopher who devoted his life to the interpretation of Spinoza's life and philosophy, writes:

Spinoza learned daily the tragic history and suffering of his people. There was hardly a family in Amsterdam which did not count many of its members or ancestors as martyrs. Many of those who had come to Amsterdam as Marranos had spent agonizing years in the prisons of the Inquisition. Mennaseh ben Israel, Spinoza's teacher, arrived in Amsterdam with his body severely maimed by torture. . . . every household in the Joodenbuurt recited bloody stories of inhuman suffering. . . . the lessons Spinoza learned from all this were only too clear. . . . He learned of the unspeakable consequences of intolerance and hatred. . . . and of the victory of the spirit over brutal force. . . . and utmost contempt for the kind of pious fanaticism which had forced his people to embrace a faith in which they could not believe.

The young Spinoza attended the famous Marrano school, which required punctual and regular attendance from eight to eleven in the morning and from two to five in the afternoon. The "free time" had to be used for preparing for the difficult classes. The teachers were scholars of international reputation. Three of them had a great influence on Baruch Spinoza: Isaac Aboab de Fonseca was the scion of a famous Marrano family. A poet and scholar, he was also a student of the Cabala and a secret believer in the Messianic movement of Shabtai Zvi, the false Messiah. For a while he was the rabbi of the Jewish community of Pernambuco, Brazil, and, as such, he was the first rabbi in the New World. Another teacher was Saul Levi Morteira, an Italian Jew, brought up by Marrano parents. In addition to being a teacher, he was a member of the Beth Din, the Jewish court which excommunicated Spinoza. The third, the most colorful and the best-known of his teachers and also a member of the court, was Manasseh ben Israel, a Marrano who was born Manoel Dias Soeiro.

Baruch Spinoza was an extraordinary student. That he mastered the Bible and its medieval commentaries can be taken for granted, but his main interest was philosophy. His own philosophical system was to be profoundly influenced by the medieval Jewish philosophers whose works he studied as a young boy in the Marrano school. All of them were Sephardic Jews whose philosophies had been largely determined by the Greeks, particularly Aristotle and Plato. The most famous of these Jewish thinkers, Moses Maimonides, applied the rational principles of Aristotle to traditional Judaism and had accepted reason as the yardstick, even for theological notions. Although he had lived in the twelfth century, Maimonides' system was not in conflict with the rationalism of Descartes which was so influential in the developing Renaissance three hundred years later. But for all its excellence, the curriculum of the Marrano school included neither the philosophy of Descartes nor any courses in the natural sciences. For this, Spinoza had to look elsewhere.

He began to attend private classes given by Franciscus van den Enden, an ex-Jesuit, physician, philologist, diplomat and bookseller who was to become his lifelong friend as well as his teacher. Van den Enden was a member of a freethinking Christian sect, the Collegiants, who worshiped without clergy or ritual. With his hunchbacked daughter Clara he taught Spinoza mathematics, physics, mechanics, astronomy, chemistry and medicine. Spinoza also learned Latin at Van den Enden's school, with Clara as his special tutor.

As he began to expand his intellectual horizons and give expression to his developing ideas, Spinoza attracted a circle of disciples, not merely among Jewish but even more among Christian intellectuals. With several members of the Collegiants, Spinoza began his intensive study of Descartes which culminated in his first published work. But even before any of his writings had been published, the number of his students grew, drawn perhaps as much to Spinoza the man as they were to his ideas.

When he was still a student at the Marrano school Spinoza had studied the writings of the twelfth-century Jewish philosopher Abraham Ibn Ezra, in which he read the sentences that became the cornerstone of his thinking: "God is the One who is the All. He is in everything and everything is in Him." Spinoza interpreted these statements as a kind of pantheistic theology which had little in common with the stern monotheism of Jewish Orthodoxy. To Spinoza, "He is in everything" meant a God-centered universe in which God was identical with Nature. His God was neither the God of the Church nor of the Synagogue. It was not a God who needed prayer or demanded ritual. Spinoza's God was the "center of all things," not the director of an institution.

Spinoza had become a "God-intoxicated man." Later, philosophers spoke in admiration about his mathematical system, but the real source of Spinoza's philosophy was his idea of God. His *Tractatus Theologico-Politicus* was the first attempt ever made at a critical analysis of the Bible. It was not published until after his excommunication (anonymously), but it contained the religious creed which he espoused to his students and which was considered heretical: "All our knowledge and our certainties depend solely upon our recognition of God's existence. If we had no clear conception of God, we must begin to doubt everything. The more we understand Nature, the more complete is our understanding of God. Our most precious possession is cognition and understanding. Our happiness depends upon our knowledge of God. But cognition is *amor dei*, the love of God."

In a man of such profound piety, the ban must have

evoked nothing but pity for the religious bureaucracy of a community of men of very small stature. Indeed, it is hard to understand why Spinoza, so profoundly influenced by his Jewish heritage, should have been subjected to excommunication. As a matter of fact, by the time the ban was pronounced on Spinoza, it had lost its significance in most Jewish communities. Only in Amsterdam, which still walked the treacherously narrow line between its Catholic past and its newly acquired Jewish present, was it still in force.

By 1655 the reputation of Spinoza as a teacher had spread. It is said that several of his Jewish students testified about his teachings to the Jewish community, but this cannot be proved. It was also rumored that the community offered him a stipend for life if he would retire to a quiet place to think by himself and discontinue the meetings with the students. It was not only the teaching of what they considered heresy that disturbed the Orthodox minds; it was the additional fear that Spinoza's pantheistic idea of God and his critical analysis of Scripture would create Christian animosity against the young and insecure Jewish community. There were even whispered reports about an attempt on Spinoza's life instigated by the Jewish community, but for this, also, we have no documentary proof. We only know that Spinoza would not have accepted the stipend or been frightened by the assassination attempt.

All during 1655 the heads of the community met with their spiritual leaders to consider what could be done in the face of the growing danger of a heresy more alarming even than Da Costa's. Spinoza was the most brilliant of their students, the son of one of the most active and highly respected members of the congregation. For the two scholars who were members of the religious court, Isaac Aboab de Fonseca and Manasseh ben Israel, both proud of their most promising student, it must have been an agonizing and conscience-ridden battle. But the decision was finally made.

Ironically, during the year just preceding his excommunication, Spinoza had faithfully observed the period of mourning for his father. Although he had come to the conclusion that neither ritual nor institutionalized religion had any validity, for twelve months he daily attended the services of the congregation to say Kaddish, the prayer for the dead, because his father would have wanted it. In the Book of Contributions of the Jewish community of Amsterdam can still be found the entry: "On the fifth day of December 1655, the Sabbath of the Hanukkah festival, Baruch Spinoza contributed six placas [pennies]."

The excommunication ban freed Spinoza from the burden of such religious responsibilities. He could now devote his life to philosophy. To him loneliness and banishment meant serenity and peace and time to work. He lived for a short time among his Collegiant friends in Ouwerkerk, a village south of Amsterdam, taught in Van den Enden's school, and began to write the philosophical books which have earned him immortality.

He received several other offers to teach. The Elector Palatine offered him a professorship at the University of Heidelberg at a salary which must have seemed a fortune to the impoverished Spinoza. Because the condition for this great honor was that Spinoza, free in everything, should refrain from attacking the teachings of "the official religion prevailing in our realm," he refused the post. When Louis XIV invited him to the court of Versailles to be the resident philosopher of the royal household, Spinoza declined the honor. He preferred peace and demanded complete freedom. He had learned how to grind optical lenses, an occupation guaranteeing a small compensation. But it was a profession that may have hastened the end of his life because the fine dust from the lenses aggravated an inherited tendency toward tuberculosis, the disease to which he finally succumbed.

After leaving Ouwerkerk he returned to Amsterdam, and in 1660 he left his native city. He spent the next three years in Rijnsburg, headquarters of the Collegiants, and then moved to Voorburg, near The Hague. In 1670 he moved to The Hague, and the following year he rented a room in the house of Hendryk van der Spyck in that city. This was to be his last home. In spite of the fact that very little was published under his own name during his lifetime, he had become one of the sages of the day. Though he had a collection of one hundred and eleven books, his rooms were humble and bore no physical resemblance to the elegant salons of the rich Jewish ladies of eighteenth-century Berlin who attracted the intellectuals of their time. Still, wherever he lived, the thinkers, philosophers and statesmen, and even members of high society came to visit and pay homage to him. Copies of his early writings circulated in Holland and abroad.

Even the Christian Church, in at least twenty synods, issued violent reprimands against Spinoza. His *Tractatus*, which appeared only under his initials, was known to be the work of "the unspeakable Jewish heretic Baruch Spinoza." But he remained calm and even entered into a philosophical correspondence with one of his most severe critics whom he assured of his great esteem and understanding. Yet he was not, as some people depicted him, a man eager to please and ready to forgive. In his later life he often displayed the fire of his convictions and a readiness to fight for them. When, in 1672, French armies occupied the Netherlands, he participated fearlessly in several political battles, and when his friend the great Dutch statesman John de Witt was killed by a mob in the street, the quiet philosopher had to be restrained from marching against them with a placard on his shoulders denouncing tyranny and violence and mob rule. He was certainly a quiet man, but he was not meek. And to the end of his life he remained a God-intoxicated man.

Spinoza died in 1677. His body was interred in the cemetery of the New Church on the Spuy. Six carriages followed the hearse with many well-known personages in them. The receipt for the funeral read: "On February 25, 1677, Benedictus Spinoza was buried. The fee amounts to 20 gilders. It was paid."

The list of his personal belongings after his death is the most moving and probably the most graphic description of his incredible modesty: a bedstead, an old Turkish robe, a few pairs of socks (several in need of mending), two pairs of shoes. No bank account, no cash. He had always said that he just wanted to earn enough to pay his rent, to feed his body and to leave enough money for his funeral expenses. But there was not enough money to buy a grave, and so he was interred in a "rented grave" where six persons had previously been buried. There is no marker, certainly no tombstone. He is memorialized by his philosophy, the only monument he could afford.

Spinoza had lived all his life as a Marrano, a man between two worlds. He could not accept the medieval world which the Marranos of Amsterdam had chosen at a time when new ideas—the philosophies of the Renaissance and the new humanism of the century—were flourishing in the world. Nor did Christianity, to which his forefathers had succumbed in Spain, satisfy his yearning for truth and justice. He was buried in a Christian cemetery without any clerical attendance. No final blessing was said. He died as he had lived for most of his life—neither Christian nor Jew.

Both Spinoza and Da Costa felt compelled to verbalize their religious doubts and were prepared to fight for their convictions. Many others among the returning Marranos must have thought as they did, but rather than address the religious problem directly, they preferred to show their modernity in their professions, in the natural sciences, literature, medicine and international trade. If they were disappointed not to have found in the new Marrano communities a religious echo of the intellectual and spiritual atmosphere of the seventeenth century, they did not express it.

The most profoundly tragic aspect of the stories of Da Costa and Spinoza lies in the failure of the Jewish community to come to terms with the ideas which they represented. One might have expected the Jewish community, which so loved scholarship and philosophy, to have gained from the intellectual accomplishments of Da Costa and Spinoza. The rabbinical leaders of Amsterdam, Hamburg, Venice, and all the other places of Marrano refuge might indeed have stimulated the beginning of modern Jewish history and applied the questioning spirit of the times to Judaism. They could have saved many of their intellectuals the doubt which separated them from the Jewish community. They could have absorbed Spinoza's pantheism and Da Costa's criticism within a new interpretation of the Jewish tradition. Had they done so, Sephardic Judaism might have assumed a new spiritual leadership of the Jewish world, and had they prevailed they would have emerged as a new creative force, the forerunners of Moses Mendelssohn and the movement of enlightenment which developed much later, in eighteenth-century Germany. Instead, they succumbed to the obscurantism of Vilna and they set the tone for the Sephardic Judaism of the future.

To this day there is no Sephardic synagogue which is not strictly Orthodox. Although not all Sephardic Jews are personally Orthodox, Orthodoxy has remained the official Sephardic tradition. Nowhere in the entire Sephardic world has Reform or Conservative Judaism penetrated. It is as if they are still fearful of any deviation which would undermine their no longer newly established Jewish faith. And although they still retain some, almost unconscious vestiges of the Church—such as the kiss thrown to the ark —they cannot condone any more obvious references or similarities to the Church under whose shadow they lived for so long.

Perhaps an anecdote will illustrate the impact their history in Spain still has on present-day descendants of the Marranos. I was once invited to preach in the main Sephardic synagogue in Sarajevo, Yugoslavia. I was sitting next to the chief rabbi on the platform before the altar, waiting for the service to begin at the scheduled time. However, although two thousand people had filled the beautiful temple, nothing happened. After a long while I turned to my colleague and asked the reason for the uncommon delay. He replied, with some embarrassment, that I was sitting before the altar with my legs crossed, and that reminded the Sephardic community of the Cross which their ancestors had been forced to worship many centuries before. It was a great relief to the rabbi and the congregants when I uncrossed my legs. The service began. They were no longer "in the shadow of the Cross."

Chapter Four

Much has been written about the religion of the Marranos in Spain and Portugal. The description of their brand of Judaism includes the list of Jewish customs which they remembered, the special prayers which they said, and the few holidays which they still, furtively, commemorated. Yet one important element of their religion has not been sufficiently stressed: their belief in the coming of the Messiah.

Although the idea that the Messiah is still to come is an essential part of Jewish doctrine and is the reason for the Jewish rejection of Jesus as Christ—the Messiah—it found a more fervent acceptance among Sephardic Jews than among Ashkenazim. (There have been something like ten Messianic movements in Jewish history, and not a single one was led by an East European Jew.) Among the Marranos it became a central belief and a hope for the immediate future. In fact, the idea of the imminent arrival of the Messiah was never far removed from their actual life, and they seem to have been almost obsessed by the notion that he might be just around the corner. Gerson Cohen, the

Jewish medievalist, claims that this Marranic belief may account for the many conversions among Spanish Jews, who perhaps counted on the Messiah to rescue them from their conversion. Anything between the present and the Messianic tomorrow was thought to be just an episode. The Marranos' hope for the Messiah was so well known that the Spanish verb *esperar* ("to hope") became a catchword in the sixteenth-century Spanish drama to identify the character who was of Jewish descent. *"Esperanza* is the Jewish characteristic par excellence, and the satiric use of such terms is a leitmotif in the Spanish drama of the Golden Age."

Not satisfied with traditional Jewish concepts of the Messiah myth, the Spanish Jews created their own unique version of the Messianic prophecy. "When the Messiah comes to Spain," they said, "he will arrive in the guise of a fish, for if he appeared as a man the Inquisition would catch and burn him. As a fish he will enter by swimming up the river Tajo and then accomplish redemption." Like the Marrano himself, the Messiah had to be a Jew in an elaborate disguise. A famous Marrano physician and mystic, Abraham Cardoso, took the analogy one step further when he wrote: "It is ordained that the king Messiah don the garments of a Marrano and so go unrecognized by his fellow Jews. In a word, it is ordained that he become a Marrano like me."

The reasons for the attraction the Marranos felt for the Messianic vision are complicated and open to speculation. Perhaps one factor was the Sephardic contact with the non-Jewish world. As we have noted, the Ashkenazi's life inside the ghetto permitted him to cultivate his Jewish beliefs without regard to the religious practices of those outside the walls. The Sephardi, living among those who believed that the Messiah—Christ or Mohammed—had already come, may have felt a need to reiterate with equal fervor his own contention that his Messiah was still expected, and might have added, somewhat defensively, that he might indeed come tomorrow. Whatever the reason, the fact remains that Marranic expectations of a very special kind were at the core of the Marranic version of Judaism, and as such are an important aspect of the anatomy of the secret Jew. In fact, the influence of this belief is still noticeable in the Marranos of the present day, and it had an impact on the history of the crypto-Jew.

Because of this Messianic obsession, it is no wonder that several individuals pretending to be the Messiah found immediate acceptance among the Marranos. In the early days of the Portuguese Inquisition, for example, a poor, uneducated New Christian tailor named Luis Diaz, remembering the Messianic tales which he had heard from his Jewish parents, came to the conclusion that he not only had prophetic gifts but was, in fact, the promised Messiah. He was looked up to with reverence by his fellow New Christians, both in his native town of Setúbal and in Lisbon, which he frequently visited. Wherever he went he was treated with extravagant signs of respect, his followers kissing his hands devoutly when they encountered him in the street. In the end, however, he was executed by the Inquisition.

In 1524, an adventurer named David Reubeni appeared in Venice, claiming to be the son of a Jewish king. The Marranos there, and later in Rome, eagerly welcomed him as the forerunner of the Messiah, who, in the prophecy, is supposed to be heralded by the appearance of a descendant of the Biblical King David.

In the seventeenth century the Marrano's Messianic longing became especially strong and had important consequences. During this period, Messiah fever infected not only Jews but also Christians who were predicting the second coming of Christ. The Millennium, reckoned by Christian mystics from the time of Jesus' birth, was at hand. The Thirty Years' War had left much of Europe devastated, hungry and hopeless; though religious in its origins, it had brought nothing but misery to the people. Moreover, the Church, all-embracing and universal, was now split by the Reformation and was no longer the rock of comfort it had once been. It was a good time for mysticism, since nothing else seemed to offer solutions, and the suffering which was traditionally expected to precede the coming of the Messiah was all too visible. All over Europe men claimed to have the answers. The leading mystic of the time was Jacob Boehm, a Silesian shoemaker, who was wrestling with the problem of evil. In England a Puritan sect whose members called themselves the Men of the Fifth Monarchy had great influence while they waited for Christ to return to earth. The Messianic yearnings of the Marranos of Amsterdam, Antwerp, Hamburg, Bayonne and Venice were in tune with the times.

The Messianic dream was not exclusively the property of crackpots and charlatans. It found an important expression in one of Spinoza's most eminent teachers, Manasseh ben Israel, a Marrano, born as a Christian in Lisbon, and circumcised and converted to Judaism in Amsterdam. The face of ben Israel, preserved in several engravings and in a portrait by Rembrandt, conveys little: a Vandyke beard and small, almost Oriental, eyes; a rather empty and commonplace face. Even such a genius as Rembrandt, whose portraits were so revealing, apparently discovered nothing extraordinary in the features of his friend Manasseh. He may indeed have been a talented teacher, but he was neither a significant philosopher nor a great theologian; and although he wrote a great deal, there was little which was noteworthy. Besides being a rabbi, he was a successful businessman, supplementing his meager earnings as the spiritual leader of the famous Amsterdam synagogue of Neveh Shalom (Paths of Peace) by engaging in trade with relatives in Brazil. He also founded the first Hebrew printing press in Holland, which for two centuries thereafter was the world's center for Jewish book publishing.

In spite of his apparent mediocrity, ben Israel attracted many of the greats of his time and corresponded with important people, not only in the Netherlands but beyond its borders. Today he would probably be remembered only as Spinoza's teacher were it not for the fact that he was that rare combination of fanatic mystic (and a fervent believer in the coming of the Messiah) and practical politician. Seldom have political acumen and theology been so harmoniously wedded. These qualities established Manasseh ben Israel in Jewish history as the man who made possible the return of the Jews to England, a country from which they had been expelled in 1290 by Edward I.

To Manasseh ben Israel, the demographic distribution of the Jews over the globe was of great Messianic significance. In the last chapter of the Book of Daniel, which deals in mysterious terms with the time appointed for the resurrection and the coming of the Messiah, it is written that the knowledge of the last days of mankind (when the Messiah will come) are to be "kept a secret and the book would be shut as a secret till the crisis at the end; ere then many shall give way and trouble shall be multiplied on earth." But when will it be? When will the Messiah come? The answer in Daniel's cryptic language is: "When the power of Him who scattered the sacred people should be over, then the end of all should arrive." In the mystical interpretation, the Prophet seemed to say that the Messiah could not come unless the "sacred people," the Jews, were actually scattered all over the world, until there would be no country without Jews.

Manasseh ben Israel had read a report by Antonio de Montezinos, a Marrano, describing a strange discovery he had made in America. In a sworn affidavit to the Jewish community of Amsterdam he told about some Indians he had met in Quitó, Ecuador, who were familiar with Jewish customs and who claimed to be descendants of the ancient Hebrew tribes of Reuben and Levi. Since De Montezinos was a well-known globetrotter, his report was received with the greatest respect, and Manasseh ben Israel considered it so important that he repeated it in his pamphlet "The Hope of Israel," published in 1650. Only four years later twenty-four Portuguese Jews landed in New Amsterdam (later to be named New York) to become the first Jewish settlers in North America. The Jewish presence on the South and North American continents meant that there was now only one country where Jews could not live. The fact that they were still barred from England seemed to be the only factor preventing the Messiah from fulfilling the prophecy of Daniel. Therefore, it became Manasseh's personal crusade to open England to Jewish immigration.

England was in turmoil. Charles I had been executed, and for the first time in her history, England was a republic under the leadership of the extraordinary Lord Protector

Oliver Cromwell. The public execution of a beloved king created an atmosphere of moral uneasiness among the people, and the religious issues of Presbyterianism versus Catholicism favored the development of mystical movements in the country. There was an Old Testament flavor to some of these religious movements which favored Judaism over any of the Christian denominations. A few of the believers in these sects even went to Holland and converted to Judaism.

Although there was a small community of Marranos who had come to England in the sixteenth century, they, naturally, did not profess Judaism openly. In London they formed a distinctive group of about one hundred, married within their own community and held Jewish services secretly in their rather sumptuous homes. Almost all of them were well-to-do, some of them very rich. Among them was Antonio Fernandez Caravajal, one of the richest men in England. He had acquired a large fortune in the Canary Islands, and owned a fleet of merchant ships which was used for his far-flung commercial interests in the new East and West Indian territories, in South America and in the Levant. He had arrived from Portugal in 1630, and unlike his fellow Marranos, is said to have practiced Judaism openly. In a reported conversation with a Franciscan monk, he is quoted as saying, "Don Mathias, although I am a Jew, we shall meet in heaven." To Cromwell, Caravajal and his fellow Marranos were indispensable. Burton, a contemporary writer of a "parliamentary diary" speaks of "The Jews [he means the English Marranos], those able and general in intelligence, whose intercourse with the continent Cromwell had before turned to a profitable account."

If Manasseh ben Israel knew about the English Marranos

—and there is no evidence he did—he probably discounted their importance. In the early 1650s he had planned to travel to England to submit a plea for readmission of his people, but he became ill and his relative, Manuel Martínez Dormido, went in his behalf. When the appeal was turned down, Dormido insisted that Manasseh be invited to submit his petition in person, and a commission appointed by Cromwell was to consider the matter of the Jews' readmission.

The commercial intercourse between England and Holland was bringing many Englishmen to Amsterdam, and ben Israel was already known in England. It is known that Queen Henrietta Maria, consort of Charles I, had visited the Amsterdam synagogue in which ben Israel preached and that his welcoming speech was delivered in English. It was difficult to refuse permission for his visit to England, so ben Israel's petition for the readmittance of his people was officially submitted in 1655. A few paragraphs from this document will indicate the thrust of his request:

These are the boons and the favor which I, Manasseh ben Israel, in the name of my Hebrew nation, beseech of your most serene Highness, and may God prosper you and give you much success in all your undertakings. Such is the wish and desire of your humble servant.

The first thing which I ask of your Highness is that our Hebrew nation be received and admitted into this mighty Republic under the protection and care of your Highness. . . . that it please your Highness to allow us public synagogues, not only in England, but also in all other conquered places which are under the power of your Highness, and to allow us to exercise our religion in all details as we should, that we should be allowed to have a plot or cemetery outside the city for burying our dead without being molested by anyone.

Ben Israel's welcome in London was, in reality, merely an act of courtesy. Cromwell was favorably disposed toward his position and actually had made up his mind to readmit the Jews before the plea was made. His experience with the Marranos, not merely as traders but as a source of political and military information, had been most satisfactory. It stood to reason that the Jews, whose relatives were scattered all over the globe and whose relationship with Spain and Portugal were still intact, could furnish the most reliable intelligence about events in the rest of the world. Some Spanish and Portuguese Marranos, ostensibly Christians but practicing Jews in reality and observing Jewish customs in their homes, even held important positions—for instance, the Marquis of Niza, a Marrano and a great admirer of Manasseh ben Israel, was Portugal's ambassador to France.

So when the commission made a statement indicating that there was no legal obstacle to a return of the Jews, since no legal document prohibiting this had been found, it was quite sufficient for Cromwell. His final decision was that "the Jews deserving it, may be admitted into this nation to trade and traffic and to dwell among us as Providence shall give occasion, so long as they make no parade of their religion."

Winston Churchill, in his *History of the English-Speaking Peoples*, offers this sober analysis of Cromwell's reasons for the admission of the Jews: "Religious toleration challenged all the beliefs of Cromwell's days and found its best friend in the Lord Protector himself. Believing the Jews to be a useful element in the civic community he opened again to them the gates of England which Edward had closed four hundred years before. There was in practice comparatively little persecution on purely political grounds and even Catholics were not seriously molested. A man who in that bitter age could write 'We look for no compulsion but that of light and reason' and who could dream of a union and a right understanding embracing Jews and Gentiles cannot be wholly barred from his place in the forward march of liberal ideas." No general history of England ever mentions Manasseh ben Israel and his role in this turning point in the history of English Jewry.

After a year in London, ben Israel was granted an annual stipend of one hundred pounds. Although his mission had succeeded and his petition had provided Cromwell with the excuse he wanted to admit the Jews to England, ben Israel was disappointed. He had wanted a solemn declaration by the Lord Protector, or at least a meeting of Parliament, which would have recognized the religious, Messiah-oriented reasons why this should be done. He wanted a proclamation heralding the coming of the Messiah now that the prophecy of Daniel had been fulfilled. Although he was a gifted political analyst, in this case his mystical goals must have blinded him to the pragmatism of the English people and to the mercantile spirit of the time which had contributed to new freedoms for Jews in many parts of the world "provided that they were ready to invest capital there."

Personal tragedy caused him additional grief. His son, who had accompanied him to England, died there. Manasseh, broken in spirit and physically ill, took his son's body home to Amsterdam. There, only a year later, he died without knowing that in reality, he had helped to open a new chapter in the history of his people. The Messiah did not come, although pseudo-Messiahs continued to spring up and attract followers, particularly among the Marranos.

The most colorful and fantastic of these was one of the most controversial figures in all of Jewish history. He was Shabtai Zvi, born in Smyrna in 1626, a few years after the start of the Thirty Years' War. Throughout his life he was imbued with an extraordinary understanding and feeling for the spirit of his times. Mysticism and tragedy formed the background and motivation of his memorable life. Its aftermath was the founding of a new Marranic community in Asia Minor.

One of the three sons of a poor father, Shabtai Zvi, because of his frail health, was elected to devote his life to the study of the mystical Cabala, an ancient Jewish theosophy which had exerted a profound effect upon Christian thought. There was never a system of Jewish thought closer to Christianity than the religious movement of the Cabala, to which many devout Jews were attracted. Although it contained some curious notions of Trinity, which some of the *conversos* of Spain had used to assert the veracity of the church fathers and the New Testament, the Cabala was not considered a heretical pursuit. It was in the pages of the Zohar, the sacred Cabalistic Bible, that converts to Christianity found a justification for their new belief in the divinity of Christ. Throughout Church history such Christian theologians as Johannes Reuchlin and Pope Leo X studied Hebrew in order to comprehend the mysteries of the Cabala.

It was natural that Shabtai Zvi should be a Cabalist, since Smyrna was one of the most important centers of this mystical movement. While still a young man, he attracted a group of scholars who gathered around him to spend endless hours in meditation on the ten S'phirot, or emanations, which, according to the Cabala, were the only means of reaching the inscrutable Ein Sof, the endlessness of God. Not merely study was required, but a kind of passion which led to ecstasy. This ecstasy, an integral part of the Cabalistic male community's worship, led to their opponents' claim that there was moral laxity among the Cabalists. (There are indeed some sexual components to the Cabalistic devotions.) In the fifty years of his life, Shabtai Zvi wavered between the total abstinence of an ascetic, almost monastic life on the one hand, and unbridled passion on the other. During the ascetic period of his early career, he divorced two wives to free himself from any kind of sexuality. Later he found it not only acceptable but desirable to marry Sarah, a young waif who had led a life of rather easy virtue in Livorno, Italy.

But meditations in a private circle in Smyrna, however profound and rapturously ecstatic, far away from the masses of the Jewish people, could not spark an international movement, and this was, clearly, what Shabtai Zvi had in mind. His hopes and personal ambitions involved the whole of the people of Israel, not just a local group in Smyrna. What was needed was an idea common to all Jews —and if it could also appeal to the Christians, so much the better. The idea that naturally presented itself to Shabtai Zvi was the ancient hope for the coming of the Messiah. As we have seen, talk of the Messiah was in the air in the seventeenth century. According to the Cabala, in one interpretive calculation, he was to appear in 1648; in certain Christian tradition, 1666 was the year of the Millennium, the year when Christ was to appear for the second time to redeem the world.

Shabtai Zvi, playing on these hopes, announced that the Messiah would indeed come soon. An event in 1648 made this an auspicious year for his proclamation. There had been a pogrom in the Ukraine which reportedly took the lives of half a million Jews. Carried out at the instigation of the Cossack leader, Bogdan Chmielnetzky, it is, to this day, remembered as one of the worst calamities in Jewish history. Shabtai announced that the Chmielnetzky pogrom and the Thirty Years' War had been the prelude of suffering which would be followed in 1666 by the coming of the Messiah. Thus, the expectation of the great and mysterious event could be shared by Christians and Jews alike. The tragedy of the Jewish massacre and the Thirty Years' War linked them in common prayer and hope.

Then Shabtai made the decisive move. He proclaimed to the world that the expected Messiah was none other than Shabtai Zvi himself. He was at that time twenty-five years old, attractive, obsessed with the Cabala, and filled with vanity and lust for power. The force of his personal magnetism and charisma evidently convinced many people that he was right.

Such ambitions called for a dramatic act that would shock all of Jewry and focus all eyes on Smyrna, home of the new prophet. The Cabalistic meetings with his friends were now frankly conspiratorial, and a plan was decided upon. In 1651 Shabtai, in front of the open ark, pronounced the name of God. Instead of using the euphemistic "Adonai," which is commonly expressed, he boldly said "Jehovah," the sacred name which was pronounced only once a year, on the High Holy Days by the High Priest in the ancient Temple in Jerusalem. Only the Messiah, proclaiming the beginning of the New Era, was permitted to pronounce this holiest of names. At the conclusion of this outrageous rite, Shabtai announced the cancellation of certain fast days, and proclaimed that all Jewish rituals would eventually be declared invalid.

The reaction to this bold and unheard-of act was immediate, and it was not restricted to Smyrna. Without benefit of modern means of communication, Shabtai's declaration was broadcast, by word of mouth, around the world. The response was not entirely favorable: Shabtai's teacher, Joseph Escapa, pronounced the *herem*, excommunicating him from the Jewish community of Smyrna. Shabtai departed for Cairo, which, for a time, became the center of his Messianic movement.

It was in Cairo that the final organization took place, complete with finances and propaganda. Financial assistance came from Raphael Joseph Chelebi, a rich Jew, treasurer of the Turkish governor of Cairo. Without Chelebi, Shabtai's movement might have remained a local incident, but with his help and the growing enthusiastic acceptance of the Jewish masses, Shabtai was hailed as the Messiah. The green Messianic flag, the symbol of the movement, was soon seen throughout Europe and the Middle East.

Shabtai devoted the next years to feverish propaganda efforts. The opposition on the part of the Orthodox chief rabbis was overcome by the fervor of Shabtai's adherents and the loyalty of his inner cabinet. There was little time left. The fateful year of 1666 was approaching rapidly. Jews everywhere were selling their properties, packing their few belongings and moving to the various harbors to wait for the Messiah to take them to Jerusalem. An example of the kind of confidence Shabtai Zvi inspired is contained in the memoirs of one of these Jewish pilgrims, a simple German woman who left her hometown of Hameln to sit on her bundles in Hamburg, waiting patiently for the Messiah she was certain would come. She writes:

Some sold all their worldly goods—their house and all that belonged to it—and hoped every day that they would be delivered. My father-in-law, peace be with him, lived in Hameln and he gave up his home there and left behind his house and court and furnishings, and many good things, and moved to the city of Hildesheim, to reside there. And he sent to us, here in Hamburg, two large barrels with all kinds of linens. And inside there was every sort of food, such as peas, beans, dried meat, and many other things to eat, plum preserves for instance, and all manner of foods that keep. For the good man, peace be with him, thought that it was quite simple to go from Hamburg straight to the Holy Land. These barrels remained in my house for over a year. Finally they grew afraid that the meat and the other things might spoil, so they wrote us to open the barrels and take out whatever there was to eat, lest the linen rot. And so it stood for about three years, and he always thought he would use it for his journey, but such was not the will of the Most High.

We know very well that it was promised to us by the Most High, and if we are completely devout, from the very depths of our hearts, and not so wicked, I am certain that the Omnipresent would have mercy upon us. If we only kept the commandment to love our neighbors as ourselves! But merciful God, how ill we keep it! The envy and senseless hatred that are betwixt us! These can make for nothing good. And yet, dear God, what you have promised us, that you will give us, in kingliness and grace. Though it delays so long in coming, because of our sins, we shall surely have it when the appointed time is come. And on this we will set our hopes, and pray to you, almighty God, that you may at last gladden us with perfect redemption.

The Messianic uproar in the Jewish world was fantastic. Wherever Shabtai appeared, he was received with such exaltation that it must have served to strengthen his own belief in himself and his mission. The passion ran particularly high among the Marranos in Amsterdam. When Shabtai came to that famous community, the people removed the holy scrolls from the synagogue and danced in the streets to the music of Spanish Jewish tunes.

Then, in the midst of this jubilation, with the sound of the music and the visions of the dancers still fresh in his memory, Shabtai made his fatal mistake. He moved on to Constantinople. Upon his arrival he was arrested by the grand vizier, who was afraid that his presence in the city would spark revolutionary upheavals among his people. Instead of leading his people on to Jerusalem, the Messiah sat in a Turkish jail.

Some people expected the movement to collapse. The humiliation of their leader—which he had not prophesied—seemed proof that his powers were not supernatural. But although some of his followers were disillusioned, the core of the movement remained faithful to him. Shabtai, declaring that prison life was unbecoming and beneath his dignity, solicited contributions from his followers. Money poured in from all over the world and was used for effectively generous bribes which permitted him to lead the life of a king in his cell. After a time he was transferred from the prison to a suite of elegantly furnished rooms. His jail became a royal court in which he lived with Sarah, who had become the female symbol of his movement as the "Messianic Bride." He received ambassadors of the movement from many countries, among them an old and learned Cabalist from Poland, Nehemiah Cohen, who had come to see for himself what kind of man and Cabalist Shabtai was. Cohen spent three days and nights with the Messiah, and came to the conclusion that Shabtai was a dangerous charlatan. Realizing that this was not merely a threat to his own people but to the whole world, since he thought Shabtai was talented and reckless enough to start a revolution, Cohen transmitted his thoughts first to the grand vizier and then to the sultan. The judgment of both of them was that Shabtai deserved to be put to death.

All this happened in 1666, which was to have been the year of Messianic redemption. Shabtai was taken to Adrianople to face the sultan, but first he met the sultan's physician, a Jew who had converted to Islam. The physician advised him to do likewise; and when Shabtai appeared before the sultan he informed the mighty ruler of his sincere desire to embrace the religion of the Prophet Mohammed and to pray to Allah instead of to the Jehovah whose name he had so solemnly, so recklessly and so effectively proclaimed only fifteen years before. The delighted sultan gave him the name of Mehmed Effendi and the honorary title of the Sultan's Doorkeeper. All thoughts of execution were apparently forgotten. Sarah and the entire entourage, blind believers in their leader's wisdom and infallibility, followed his example and also became Mohammedans. Then they all moved to Dulcingno, a seaport of what was then Montenegro (now Yugoslavia), not far from the Albanian border. There they lived as Mohammedans, but whenever possible they attended services at the local synagogue. The ambitions of the king of the Jews were forgotten, and in the hills surrounding Dulcingno, Shabtai Zvi, the Messiah of Smyrna, died at the age of fifty.

Even in death his influence did not abate. Many of his followers in Mohammedan countries converted to Islam in the belief that their master had done so only to "liberate the impure sparks inherent in Islam from their spiritual prison." In Hungary and Moravia some Jews solemnly adopted the surname of Sheps or Shoeps as proof of an unshakable belief in Shabtai. Others began to create a new set of Jewish beliefs of which they thought the master would have approved.

Among the new preachers of the movement there were Marrano fugitives from Portugal. One of them, Abraham Miguel Cardoza, preached a sort of Jewish Holy Trinity in which Shabtai was proclaimed to be the incarnation of God. A similar theology was invented by Nehemiah Hayyun and one of the most fervent "Shabtai Tzvinickes"—or Sabbatists, as they were sometimes called—Jacob Querido, together with many hundreds of others, followed the master's example by going to the mosque to be converted to Islam. In December 1686, more than three hundred families converted to Islam in Salonika. Like Shabtai and other Marranos, they continued to attend Jewish services secretly and observed certain Jewish customs in their homes.

This was the origin of the most important group, numerically and historically, of Islamic Marranos. The faithful Mohammedans call these hidden Jews *doenmehs*, the renegades. They called themselves *ma'aminim*, the true believers. To traditional Jews, whose rejection of Shabtai Zvi and his movement was now fully vindicated, they remained *kofrim*, traitors. Over the years the *doenmeh* movement became firmly established in Asia Minor. In the nineteenth century the sect was estimated to have twenty thousand members. Salonika remained its main seat until that city became Greek in 1913. Although the Jewish community remained there under Greek rule, the *doenmehs* moved to Constantinople.

In Salonika in the early days of the movement the ten commandments "of our Lord King and Messiah Shabtai

Zvi" were proclaimed by the *doenmehs*. They still form the credo of the surviving *doenmehs* of our time.

I believe in the one and only God.

I believe in his Messiah, the true redeemer, our king Shabtai Zvi, descended from King David.

I swear not to take the name of God or his Messiah in vain and not to take an oath in their name.

I take upon myself to carry the message of the mysteries of our Messianic faith from one community to another.

I shall assemble with my fellow believers on the sixteenth day of the month of Kislev to discuss with them the secrets of our Messianic faith. [This is the month during which Shabtai had announced his Messiahship.]

I swear that I shall never convert anybody to the faith of the Turban, called Islam.

Daily will I read in the Book of Psalms.

I shall meticulously adhere to the customs of the Turks so as not to arouse their suspicion. I shall not only observe the Fast of Ramadan but all the other Muslim customs which are observed in public.

I shall not marry into a Muslim family nor maintain any intimate association with them, for they are to us an abomination and particularly their women.

I shall circumcise my sons.

To this day, *doenmehs* assemble for prayers in their own house of worship in Istanbul. Some of the devotions are still said in Hebrew and Aramaic, but most of them are recited in Ladino, the "Yiddish" of the Sephardic Jew. Although at the beginning of the movement the male children were circumcised on the eighth day after birth, as is the Jewish practice, circumcision now takes place on the third birthday of the child. The Sabbath is not commemorated, but several new festivals have been added. One of these is the ninth of Av (a day of fast in the traditional Jewish calendar, where it is remembered as the day of the destruction of the Temple in Jerusalem), which among the *doenmehs* has been chosen as the birthday of Shabtai Zvi and is commemorated with great hilarity and merrymaking. Because a roasted lamb is specifically prepared as the main dish, the celebration is called the Festival of the Lamb. Sexual laxity, a feature of the movement's early days, continues to prevail among the *doenmehs,* and the celebration of Shabtai's birthday usually ends in a sexual orgy. After the lamb is eaten, the candles are extinguished and a common exchange of wives takes place. Children born of such unions are regarded as saintly, conceived in a mysterious way as children of the holy Messiah Shabtai Zvi, who is believed to have been present at the moment of this holy intercourse.

With this disregard for the traditional Jewish chastity, it is no wonder that the book of the Bible the *doenmehs* regard most highly, and read most assiduously, is the Song of Songs. In the eighteenth century Dervish Effendi, who followed the epileptic Chonio as the leader of the Salonika *doenmeh* community, tried to eliminate marriage altogether as an institution unworthy of the sainted memory of Shabtai. Sarah, the harlot of Livorno and the Messianic bride, was still remembered as the great example of ideal womanhood. But the Jewish heritage of the *doenmehs* proved too strong, and the Festival of the Lamb remains their only official concession to free love as a religious doctrine.

From time to time the Turkish governors of Salonika,

who received complaints about the sect from the Mohammedan clergy, tried to investigate the strange existence of
the *doenmehs.* Their clannishness, their refusal to mingle
with Mohammedan families, and their marital restrictions
had become a well-known fact, difficult to hide from the
majority of the people among whom they had lived for
many generations. Socially, they seemed impenetrable, although in their Moslem religious practices they were beyond reproach. In fact, they often seemed even more devout followers of the Prophet Mohammed and more sincere
worshipers of Allah than the rest of the community. They
fasted during Ramadan, and their leaders and adherents
were found in large, even conspicuous numbers among the
pilgrims to Mecca. It was well known that in the seventeenth century Joseph Zvi, one of the immediate followers
of Shabtai Zvi and one of his inner circle, died on the way
from his pilgrimage to Mecca, and the day of his death is
still commemorated.

Nevertheless, there were some indications to the outside
community that all was not what it seemed and that the
Islamic faith of the *doenmehs* was a little too obviously and
purposefully observed. In most cases, large contributions
to the governor's private purse prevented a closer investigation. However, in 1859 Husni Pasha, then governor of
Salonika, investigated thoroughly and found a *doenmeh*
school system where a special brand of Islam was taught.
As a result, the schools were closed. Thereafter, greater
caution and secrecy were imposed by the Sabbatists, and
the sect remained intact.

Another investigation, the final inquiry, took place in
1875 under Governor Nehdad. The resulting memorandum
submitted to the Turkish government praised the *doenmehs*

for their industry and high moral standards. By then the *doenmehs* had become highly respected and were an important civic factor in the community. They were bright, industrious and successful in the world of business and in the professions. Yet during the investigation no one had succeeded in attending their private prayer meetings, no one had heard their Hebrew and Ladino songs, and certainly no outsider was admitted to witness the celebration of Shabtai's birthday. The Festival of the Lamb remained the secret of all secrets.

The revolt of the Young Turks in 1908 against the authoritarian regime of Sultan Abdul Hamid began among the intellectuals of Salonika. It was from there that the demand for a constitutional regime originated. Among the leaders of the revolution which resulted in a more modern government in Turkey were Djavid Bey and Mustafa Kemal. Both were ardent *doenmehs*. Djavid Bey became minister of finance; Mustafa Kemal became the leader of the new regime and he adopted the name of Atatürk. His opponents tried to use his *doenmeh* background to unseat him, but without success. Too many of the Young Turks in the newly formed revolutionary Cabinet prayed to Allah, but had as their real prophet Shabtai Zvi, the Messiah of Smyrna.

Messiah fevers continued to infect the Marranos. Perhaps the most bizarre case involved Jacob Frank, who was born in Russia in 1723. By the time of his death, in 1791, he had managed to convert from Judaism to Islam and then to Christianity, carrying many thousands of followers with him in his religious exultations and peregrinations.

Convinced that he was the heir to Shabtai Zvi's Messianic role, he converted to Islam hoping to attract the *doenmeh*

Marranos as his followers. When this scheme for leadership did not succeed, he embarked on a pilgrimage through Eastern Europe, picking up the followers of Shabtai Zvi as he went. By the time he arrived in Poland, he had a considerable retinue of devotees, who thought of God as the Holy Father, of Frank as the Holy King and of his wife as the Holy Matron.

This sect took the Cabala as their Holy Book, thereby incurring the wrath of the traditional Jewish community which obviously would take umbrage at this supplanting of the Talmud as the book by which Jews lived. Nor were the community relations of the Frankists helped by their practice of dancing naked in mixed groups, by their wife-swapping, and by other similar licentious customs. It was for these transgressions, utterly shocking to the Jewish community, that the Frankists were finally jailed and excommunicated in 1756.

Notice of the excommunication was sent to the Polish authorities with the recommendation that the Frankists be punished by death. Undaunted, Frank himself appealed to Bishop Dembowsky, the Catholic prelate of Brody in the Ukraine. Then Frank led his followers to convert to Christianity. He led them, but he himself remained a Jew—for a time.

The infuriated Talmudists set upon these New Christians and cut off their Jewish beards. To add to their difficulties, their protector, Bishop Dembowsky, died, and the Frankists were expelled from Poland. They scattered over the continent, and two years later Frank himself turned up in Poland, where, in what must be considered a miraculous circumstance, the king became his godfather at his final conversion—to Roman Catholicism.

Whatever the motives and religious aberrations of Jacob Frank, or of his predecessor Shabtai Zvi, they can be considered two examples, albeit extreme, of that curious phenomenon, the crypto-Jewish experience.

Chapter Five

The strange story of the secret Jews cannot be understood without a consideration of the extraordinary contribution they made to the field of international commerce. Because Jewish communities existed in so many parts of the world—Europe, the Levant, the countries of the Far East, and by the seventeenth century, in the New World—Marranos were presented with natural opportunities to participate in international trade. Language barriers were easily overcome, since all Marranos spoke Spanish or Ladino, no matter how far apart they were geographically. And in a sense these commercial enterprises, which spanned so many continents, became something like a family affair in which a common heritage and religion forged bonds that were often as strong as any biological ties could have been. After the discovery of the New World, the descendants of the rich Spanish Jewish families, who had financed the voyages of Christopher Columbus and contributed (sometimes through the Inquisition's confiscation) to the treasuries of the princes of Aragon, began to play a pivotal role in the development of the new capitalism. And when international commerce became the main source of income, particularly for those countries whose explorers had discovered new sources of gold, spices and other riches, the Marranos became deeply involved in the exploitation of the new markets.

Early in the sixteenth century, Portugal had moved into the forefront of international commerce. Her famous navigator Vasco da Gama had reached India in the spring of 1498 through a new route—around the Cape of Good Hope. This event transformed Portugal from a second-rate nation to the leading seafaring country of the century—at a time when twenty percent of its population was Jewish. Many of these were secret Jews, Marranos, refugees from the Spanish Inquisition. It is not surprising that upon their immigration to Portugal they pursued their previous occupations. A contemporary source lists them as "cobblers, bakers, tanners, soap makers, tailors, hatters, cloth manufacturers, builders and metal craftsmen." In the professions they were so predominant that "physician," "astrologer," "mathematician" and "alchemist" were virtually synonymous with the word "Jew." The *conversos* were mostly members of the middle class, yet the number of rich families was considerable, and they played a significant role in the early capitalist ventures on which their adopted country embarked in the sixteenth century.

Some of the richest of the Portuguese Marranos were able to establish branches of their enterprises in England and on the Continent, and many ventured into the New World to take advantage of the extraordinary opportunities for their diversified commercial undertakings. As their number abroad swelled, especially after the Inquisition reached Portugal, the term "Portuguese Merchants" was the name applied, tongue in cheek, to those *conversos* who had left Portugal and established businesses in other countries. They maintained official membership in the Church, but they were usually known to be Marranos and were often able to practice their religion more or less openly. Their contribution to the commercial well-being of a town or even a country protected them from expulsion and persecution.

The wealth of these Portuguese immigrants, according to figures which have come down to us, was staggering. In France there were Marrano settlements in Bordeaux, Avignon, Nantes and Marseilles, and it became a compliment to a Christian businessman in these cities to characterize him as being *"riche comme un juif."* In England, as we have seen, there were, in the early seventeenth century, only about one hundred Marrano families, but they were among the most successful merchants of London. In Germany, forty Marrano families participated in founding the Bank of Hamburg in 1619, and by the middle of that century they were accused of having too luxurious a life style, as evidenced by their palatial homes and their ostentatious funerals and weddings. The fortune of the Marranos of Altona, near Hamburg, was estimated at almost six million marks, and some of the finest homes in Amsterdam belonged to newly arrived Marranos.

The affluence of many of the Marrano families was derived from their commerce with the new Americas. It is known that six hundred Marranos left Holland for Brazil in the middle of the seventeenth century. A traveler who visited that country reported: "Among the free inhabitants of Brazil who were not in the Dutch West India Company service, the Jews were the most considerable in number.

They had come there from Holland and built stately houses in Recife. They were all traders which were of great consequence to Dutch Brazil."

Others settled in the West Indian archipelago and became deeply involved in the newly developing sugar trade. In the seventeenth century the European settlers, on the island of Barbados, were mainly Marranos who had emigrated from Holland after converting to Judaism. It was these new immigrants who introduced an improved method of refining the sugar cane which saved the island's faltering sugar industry and resulted in a prosperous market for what eventually became its main export.

In British Jamaica, the Jews were active in the cultivation and refining of sugar, and they were so valuable to the economy that when some Christian merchants asked the governor in 1681 to exclude the Jews, their petition was rejected with these unequivocal words: "I am of the opinion that His Majesty could not have more profitable subjects than the Jews and the Hollanders." By the eighteenth century the Jews were paying most of the taxes on the island of Jamaica, and both industry and international trade were in their hands.

The Marranos also settled in the Dutch island of Surinam and in the French possessions of Martinique, Guadeloupe and Santo Domingo, where they quickly became important members of the commercial establishments.

These successes in their business ventures had a far-reaching effect, for after a time, when nations began to understand the almost unlimited possibilities which the new markets opened, emigration of Marranos, who were known to be efficient and experienced in international commerce, was encouraged and enthusiastically welcomed. The French

king, Henry II, welcomed merchants "who were called
New Christians" in a proclamation which decreed that they
be "permitted to establish themselves in the realm without
being naturalized." A report to Charles V stated with satisfaction that "Portuguese merchants of Jewish origin arrived
in Marseilles and went up the River Rhone to settle and
trade in Lyons." None of the usual obstacles, none of the
traditional limitations were set. The Jews were more than
welcome and nobody cared where or how they worshiped
as long as they contributed to the economy.

Then, in 1683, the French government insisted upon a
general expulsion of the Jews from France. Special instructions were sent to the authorities of Bordeaux, which had
a considerable community of Marranos, warning them "not
to expel more than a dozen Conversos every year because
if they are forced to leave Bordeaux, it would ruin the
city's economy as the commerce is almost entirely in the
hands of that sort of persons." Those Marranos who did
have to leave France went to Santo Domingo, where a large
group of the French colonists were New Christians who
had come from Bordeaux and La Rochelle.

It should not be forgotten that these were the same people who, a few decades before their settlement in the New
World, had been victims of the Inquisition's persecution.
They had succeeded in establishing important businesses in
Portugal, accumulated considerable fortunes, and had shown
an amazing adaptability to the techniques which the new
era required. They were willing to accept the risks of new
ventures in international trade, unafraid to leave the security of the European countries for unknown and often un-
charted territories, and they exhibited a resilience and vi-
tality which was quite remarkable for a people which had

so recently been threatened by extinction in the autos-da-fé. Their commercial successes can be seen as a victory for human endurance and a tribute to the strength of the Marrano spirit.

Whenever they could they converted to Judaism, but where it was advantageous for them and the country in which they lived to be known as Christians, they were seen in church. However, no one was deceived. The "Portuguese Merchants" were known to be Jews both by origin and by conviction. Their life as Christians was just part of a grandiose masquerade in which both Christian society and the Marranos played their respective parts. If there was a Marrano wedding in a cathedral, it was common knowledge that the couple had been married in a Jewish ceremony at home before coming to the church. The second ceremony was merely a social obligation and had no religious significance whatsoever. It was a demonstration that the banking house of the father of the bride was a Christian institution with which emperors, dukes, bishops, and heads of government could safely do business. The fiction of their Christian allegiance was a business arrangement. And the Marrano subterfuge in many countries, unlike the experience of the Jews in Spain, was not fraught with danger; it was simply a social convention. Only in countries where the Inquisition was active was the Christian front maintained meticulously and Jewish customs practiced in utter secrecy.

It must be stressed that certainly thousands of the returning Marranos chose to remain Catholics and soon lost their Marranic and Jewish identity. But wherever it was possible, the majority established Jewish communities as soon as they could: in Mexico in 1528, in Curaçao in 1654, in Chile before 1570, in Cuba in the middle of the sixteenth century.

As long as Brazil was Dutch, prosperous communities of former Marranos existed in Recife, Pernambuco and Itamaraca.

Unfortunately, we have very few biographical sketches of the Marranos who lived luxuriously and often mysteriously, both on the European continent and in the New World. Their lives must have been filled with the kind of adventures we associate with people of any new frontier. But although we know quite a bit about the Jewish scholars of that time, few of the industrialists emerge as real people. There is, however, an outstanding exception: Joseph Nasi.

Several biographies of this extraordinary man exist, but no one has as yet written a novel based on his incredible life, and there is hardly a character in Jewish history who deserves a good novelist as much as he does. He was described as "an elegant chevalier, who wears a sleeveless coat, made of black Italian velvet with glittering gold buttons, a pointed golden hat such as are now in vogue, a cultured man and a brilliant conversationalist, well known in Spain, Italy, Flanders and by high ranking personalities everywhere." Joseph Nasi was, in many ways, the prototype of that new international Marrano phenomenon, the moneyed aristocrat. He was a man of many disguises and talents, a shrewd trader, a smooth diplomat, a cunning politician, a passionate lover, a Jew and Christian in happy interchangeability.

He was also a man of many names: he was called Juan Miquez in Spain, João Miguez in Portugal, Juan Michez in Germany, Michesius in Latin, and finally, when after his circumcision he emerged as a Jew, he called himself Joseph Nasi. He was born in Lisbon, probably in 1514, but he lived in Antwerp, Hamburg, Venice, Ferrara, Paris and finally Constantinople. His disguise as a Christian aristocrat was so perfect that during an investigation into his Jewish origin by the Spanish Inquisitor Ruy Fernández, the royal factor of the Spanish court wrote: "One claims that he is Jewish, which, I submit, is difficult to prove." But there was no such dispute about his wealth. A Portuguese contemporary, João de Castello Branco, stated flatly: "He is the richest man of his time." Since this was said at a time when the Fuggers in Germany had an estimated wealth of sixty-three million florins, this may have been a slight exaggeration. But the fact remains that the emperor of the Holy Roman Empire, Charles V, and his sister, regent of the Netherlands, Queen Mary, each received generous loans of two hundred florins from Nasi's bank. Huge sums were paid to the Vatican and other heads of states as bribes in many of Nasi's political interventions on behalf of his fellow Marranos in various parts of the world, for central to the life of Joseph Nasi was his constant concern for his Marrano brethren wherever they lived and a special devotion to those who needed help.

Joseph Nasi was related to the house of Mendes, one of the most active and successful banking houses in Europe, and although he had many other avocations, he was primarily a banker during his early life. It has been suggested that the Mendes family, having brought a large fortune from Spain, was admitted to Portugal under a special law which granted freedom of trade to some six hundred rich Jewish families who had converted to Catholicism but were known to live their lives as secret Jews. At any rate, at the beginning of the sixteenth century the Mendes family members lived in mansions, moved in the highest circles of the country, and the firm was regarded as the leading trading house in Portugal, with banking links to the Levantine, Asian and African trade. It had branches in many parts of the world, and the names of some of its agents in London, Venice, Ferrara, Ancona and the Netherlands are known. What was probably not known to the authorities was the fact that the agents of the house of Mendes were often engaged in illicit activities, outside their banking roles.

In fact, the agents of the house of Mendes formed a kind of international intelligence organization which relayed information about any difficulties encountered by the Marranos in the cities where they had branches. Many of the agents were themselves Marranos, but there were some bona-fide Christians among them who sent money to Marranos in distress. Whole Marrano communities received subsidies from the house of Mendes. Although it was hardly possible to conceal such considerable transfers of money from one branch to the other, nor to hide the purposes for which the money was used, the bank of Mendes was considered a Christian institution. Perhaps the fortune of the family and the complicated involvement of governments and leading families in their efforts made it possible for the authorities to ignore the Jewish descent of the family.

The head of the family, Francisco, was married to the daughter of one of the most distinguished and wealthy Spanish Jewish families, the Benveniste; for years the Benvenistes had been financial advisers to the kings of Aragon. Francisco's wife concealed her Jewishness under the adopted name of Beatrice de Luna. While Lisbon remained the headquarters of the firm, its most thriving branch was in Antwerp under the direction of Diogo Mendes, Francisco's brother.

The choice of Antwerp for the most important of the

branches of the house was not accidental, for Antwerp had become the leading harbor of Europe and surpassed all but Paris in power and wealth. More than a thousand agents in the city represented foreign banks and trading firms. As a result of the influx of foreigners, there was a housing shortage in 1530. The building housing the stock exchange had to be enlarged three times within a few decades. Five hundred ships landed in the harbor every day.

British firms, Spanish and French merchants, the German houses of Fugger, Welser and Hochstetter, as well as Spanish and Portuguese enterprises, were represented. The official policy of the authorities toward foreigners was understandably liberal, since the wealth of Antwerp depended upon them. No wonder that a royal decree of 1537 permitted *conversos* of Jewish descent to settle in Antwerp "with their children, servants and furniture, with all rights, freedom and franchises accorded to foreign merchants." It must have been well known that many of the hundreds of Marrano families who came to Antwerp, attracted by this liberal policy, would be Judaizing. In fact, there is some evidence that Diogo Mendes attended some of the clandestine services the Marranos held in the basements of their homes.

In 1539, fate suddenly altered the affairs of the house of Mendes. Francisco died in the prime of his life, leaving his young wife Beatrice de Luna and their little daughter Reyna. Though they had been married for only eight years, the vast fortune of the family, including their international business interests, was now completely controlled by Beatrice, a beautiful young woman of twenty-four, who possessed extraordinary strength and intelligence. She decided to liquidate the business in Lisbon and transfer the fortune to the branch in Antwerp. When Antwerp became the headquarters of the firm, the management continued in the capable hands of Diogo Mendes. Since all final decisions had to have Beatrice's approval, it was important for her to oversee the various business affairs and undertake the journey from Lisbon to Antwerp.

For reasons of security, it was decided that she should travel via England. She left with her infant daughter, her sister, her nephews and, most important, with Joseph Nasi (who was, of course, still called João Miguez). She also had a large entourage of servants, and as a noblewoman, she was welcomed in England by people of her social station. The mayor of Antwerp had dispatched a message to Thomas Cromwell recommending "very specially the beneficence of the king to Madame Beatrice, a lady of honor and means, sister-in-law to Sir Diogo, who, for the last twenty years had resided in the city of Antwerp, a good friend and supporter."

When the entourage arrived in Antwerp on one of the boats which made up the merchant fleet of the house of Mendes, they immediately moved into one of the great mansions of the town. After an introduction to Queen Mary, Beatrice was given a position at the court which corresponds to the present-day office of lady-in-waiting, and João Miguez held a comparable position at the court of Charles V.

On the surface, everything seemed to go well. The business was in good hands and Beatrice proved to be a prudent and shrewd administrator of one of Europe's largest fortunes. Her upbringing in a family of wealth and social graces, as well as her unusual beauty, guaranteed her acceptance in the highest social circles. Indeed she became a beloved and respected member of the community. Parties at her house were elegant and generous and attracted both nobility and money barons.

The wedding ceremony of Diogo Mendes to Beatrice's sister took place in the cathedral of Notre Dame. The Catholic rites were performed by the cardinal and two bishops, and certainly nothing could have been more Catholic. Yet we can be certain that the couple had been married according to Jewish ritual by the time they boarded the magnificent carriage that transported them to the cathedral. Under the veneer of Christian nobility they were, after all, Jews in disguise.

Despite the generally accepting climate, there *were* periods of persecution against Jews. Twice João was arrested for Judaizing, and during his stay in jail (each time for about two months) an attempt was made to confiscate the Mendes fortune. Both times he was freed by intervention of the highest authorities, Charles V and Queen Mary. An investigator into the accusation wrote: "The accused is not quite guilty of any crime. He is subject to the Emperor's decree according to which strangers who come from Portugal can stay in Antwerp as long as they please. In as far as he is concerned, an investigation in Portugal, France and Antwerp prove that he had always been a good Christian."

Yet life had become too dangerous for the family. It was true that the authorities looked the other way or imposed only mild punishments for Judaizing, but Beatrice de Luna wanted the freedom that would permit her to become a recognized, openly practicing Jew. She had wanted to leave Lisbon long before her husband died and go to a country which would free her to change her name to something more recognizably Jewish, making her dual worship at the cathedral and in the secret Marrano prayer meeting unnecessary. Even in the early years of her marriage her goal had been the Ottoman Empire. Business reasons and the protection of large interests had not permitted her to realize this dream, but now things were different. All that was needed was time to prepare her flight to Constantinople without the loss of too much of her fortune.

The trip was planned with all the care and secrecy of a conspiracy, and all precautions were taken to conceal the plan. To the outside world Doña Beatrice, lady-in-waiting to the queen, remained the same. She never missed a mass and her contributions to the Church continued to be lavish. But in the inner circle of the family and with the help of some of the oldest and most trustworthy of her servants (some of whom were also Marranos), arrangements were being carefully made over a long period of time. The first stopover on the journey was to be Venice.

But things did not go according to plan. Just as large trunks and cases filled with money and jewels were being loaded onto ships, government officers intervened and three large coffers containing immense quantities of pearls, diamonds and gold bullion were confiscated. A charge was brought against Beatrice for Judaizing and smuggling. However, she could not be found. The house, still elegantly furnished with hangings and paintings on the walls and Persian rugs on the floors, was empty. Not a single servant had been left to watch over the property.

As it transpired, Beatrice and her servants had left Antwerp allegedly to take the cure in Aix-la-Chapelle. From there the servants, more than twenty in number, all of them Portuguese, departed one by one, and in the end, Beatrice and her daughter Reyna were on their way to Venice. Upon their arrival, in 1544, they were immediately arrested as Jews, and the portion of the fortune they brought with them was confiscated.

One can be fairly certain that Beatrice did not spend the

next two years in a Venice jail. No doubt she was under house arrest, living in a fair amount of comfort. Apparently she was treated with respect and deference, probably because of the fear of international repercussions. The most important and successful diplomatic pressure came from Turkey from the sultan, Suleiman the Magnificent. He instructed his ambassador to Venice to submit to the Doges a personal message demanding the release not merely of the noble lady and her daughter, but of the confiscated property as well.

At the end of two years, Beatrice and her entourage boarded a ship which brought them to Constantinople, where four elegant carriages awaited them. Dr. Moses Mamon, the sultan's personal physician, a Jew, was in the welcoming party which the sultan had sent to pay respects to Beatrice and to her great fortune. They were escorted to their new residence which was situated "not in the neighborhood where the other Jews lived, but in a beautiful villa surrounded by gardens in the suburb of Galata for which she paid a rent of one ducat a day."

Beatrice de Luna immediately converted to Judaism and took the more simple-sounding name of Gracia Mendes which she chose because it was the Spanish version of the name Hannah, which means "grace." From then on Doña Gracia became the queen of the Marrano dispersion, generous in helping them, courageous in fighting for them, and most eager to make Constantinople, with its large Jewish community, one of the important spiritual and intellectual centers of Judaism.

Of the hundred thousand Jews in Constantinople at that time, most were Sephardim, and at least ten thousand were Marranos. Turkey had become the most secure refuge from

Christian persecutions. Muslim rulers simply could not understand Ferdinand's policy of expulsion, which, as the sultan remarked, "had impoverished Spain and enriched Turkey." The sultan could afford to be liberal. Never before, or after, had Turkey experienced so many military and economic achievements as under the rule of Suleiman the Magnificent. In a short span of time the territories now known as Hungary and Rumania had been added to her holdings, as well as Tabriz, Rhodes, Algiers, Baghdad and Aden. Suleiman was considered one of the most powerful rulers of the sixteenth century. He was prudent in his political dealings and did not hesitate to enter into alliances with "nonbelievers." While none of his predecessors would have permitted themselves to make common cause with non-Muslims, Suleiman held none of these prejudices, and made ample use of Christians and Jews. The newly arrived Mendes family was, in fact, destined to play a decisive role in his undertakings.

Shortly after his aunt, Doña Gracia, had settled in Constantinople, João Miguez arrived with a large entourage of servants and with Don Samuel, Don Abraham and Don Solomon, three other members of the family. Their arrival in one of the Mendes ships was treated as an affair of state, for it was only infrequently that a new immigrant of such splendor and such credentials settled in the capital. A contemporary writer was particularly impressed that the twenty servants were "dressed like gentlemen" and that those among them who were not Jewish had to convert and undergo the rite of circumcision. And so did João Miguez, who was at last able to discard his assumed Christian name. He became Joseph Nasi; his new name became famous not merely in Jewish but also in Turkish history.

His circumcision took place in the month of April in 1554, and in June he married his young cousin Reyna, Gracia Mendes' daughter. No longer was there any necessity for disguise. High dignitaries, including the French ambassador, attended the splendid wedding, which probably took place in the largest of the forty-five synagogues in Constantinople. The days of pretense were over. The Jewish ceremony was performed openly and all the ancient traditions were observed: the seven blessings were pronounced, the Aramaic marriage contract with its antiquated legal provisions were read, and the poor of the town received their prescribed share of charity. A new sense of freedom increased the family's joy. They had been liberated "from the yoke of slavery." When the news of the marriage reached Lisbon and Antwerp, Joseph Nasi was accused of having "betrayed his faith in order to marry a rich Jewess."

We do not know under exactly what circumstance Nasi entered the inner circle of the sultan's advisers. After Suleiman's Jewish physician introduced the family to the ruler, the sultan had to make his own judgment about the usefulness of the newcomers. There is some evidence of financial transactions having taken place between the sultan and the house of Mendes shortly after Doña Gracia's arrival, and it can be assumed that like so many other heads of state, the sultan occasionally needed more than just financial advice from the Mendes family.

The firm continued to prosper, but Joseph Nasi's main interest no longer lay in banking or importing. He became a political adviser and even, at times, an actor in the political arena. No Jew of his time, or probably of any time before the emancipation of the eighteenth century, played such an important role in world affairs. We know that he had extensive political correspondence with Maximilian II, emperor of the Holy Roman Empire, William I of Orange, and with Sigismund II, king of Poland.

But his most ingenious political dealings concerned the Marranos of the world. From his strong position in the powerful Mendes family, Joseph Nasi devised what can be called a specific Marrano strategy, a plan for economic and political revenge against those who had mistreated Marranos. The Mendes family determined that if a country or a town discriminated against Marranos, they would have to pay for it. The family had always helped individual Marranos. They had put up bail money for those in jail and sent ships for the rescue of persecuted Marranos. Now they embarked on a more ambitious plan: the ruin of those who hated them.

In more recent times some Sephardic Jews have displayed a particular talent in the field of politics. Benjamin Disraeli, the great British statesman, and Theodor Herzl, the founder of Zionism, are two illustrious examples of political thinkers whose ancestors were Sephardic Jews. But none of the Marranos of the sixteenth century had the means or the inclination of the Mendes family. It was a rare combination of money, power and piety that made their plan possible. More important, the Mendes family refused to accept the traditional role of Jewish acceptance of catastrophe and injustice as part of their fate. They were really the first Jewish activists. Not only were they unwilling to be passive about their fate, they were prepared to react forcefully in order to change it.

Two cities which became targets of the Mendes plan are known, although there must have been others: Venice and Ancona. Venice, which had become a haven of refuge for

Jews expelled from Spain, contained an ancient Jewish community dating back to the early Middle Ages. In fact, it was in Venice that the term "ghetto" was adopted to identify the Jewish quarter. The policy of the city government toward Jewish immigrants, and especially Marranos, had fluctuated. Sometimes economic considerations caused the authorities to be liberal; at other times, anti-Jewish propaganda provoked hostility. In 1550 a hostile atmosphere had prevailed, resulting in the expulsion of all Marranos. In the house of Mendes the personal experiences of Gracia Mendes, who had suffered indignities at the hands of the Venetian government for two years, had not been forgotten. Venice was listed among the enemies of the Jewish people.

When a fire destroyed much of the city's harbor in 1571, it was asserted that the house of Mendes had paid notorious arsonists to set the blaze. And while much of the city was still in flames, Joseph Nasi counseled the sultan to occupy the Venetian island of Cyprus, declaring it a Turkish possession. Later this brazen act backfired, and both the Turkish defenders and the Jews of Venice were made to suffer because it was common knowledge that it was Nasi who had been behind the scheme to occupy the island. But in the end Cyprus, the most important base of Venetian power, was in the hands of the Turks. Joseph Nasi had his revenge.

Their other plan, which had been put into effect two decades before and became known as "the Ancona Affair," had not been as successful. Ancona is an old Roman harbor city on the Adriatic, some hundred and thirty miles northeast of Rome. Its famous Romanesque church was built on the site of a temple to Venus, and still includes some columns of the ancient pagan sanctuary. In the sixteenth century Ancona was part of the Papal States, which stretched from Rome far up to the northeast, including Ferrara. The Jewish community, which dated back to the thirteenth century, depended for its well-being on the attitudes of each succeeding pope. A few of the popes had enforced the church doctrine that called for social separation and degradation of the Jews. Others had administered the Papal States as any secular government would, considering not merely spiritual values but the economic and social welfare of the people as well. Under these popes the Jewish community lived unmolested and often much favored, and Ancona's Jewish bankers and moneylenders lived very well. Occasionally special papal decrees even exempted them from wearing the badge required of all Jewish citizens. Such decrees were, of course, rewarded by generous Jewish contributions to the papal treasury.

Because the periods of freedom and liberality were more frequent than those of anti-Jewish feelings, Ancona had become a major attraction for Marranos from both Spain and Portugal. They settled there under papal protection, and with consent changed their adopted Marrano names to Jewish ones. They erected synagogues and were held in high esteem by most of the Christian community. Thus it was quite natural for the house of Mendes to establish a flourishing branch in Ancona. Gracia Mendes may even have stopped in Ancona on her way to Constantinople. Certainly she visited the city several times and knew most of the Marrano families personally.

In May 1555 the last of the benevolent popes, Julius III, died and was succeeded by Giovanni Pietro Cardinal Caraffa, a fanatic anti-Semite on whose insistence Hebrew books had been burned in Rome. As soon as Caraffa was elevated to the papacy he sent his representative to Ancona. In disregard of the assurance given to the Marranos by his predecessors, the Inquisition began in Ancona. The Marranos there, comparatively recent converts to Judaism, were considered baptized Christians and were placed under the jurisdiction of the Inquisition. Trials were held, converts were tortured, and although some were able to pay their way out of prison with enormous sums, those who could not or who refused to deny their return to Judaism died during the several autos-da-fé which were held in Ancona.

The news of the tragedy reached Gracia Mendes in the autumn of 1555. To her it was not merely another report of a Marrano tragedy, but many of the people who had been put to death were her intimate friends. The outrage of Ancona called for extraordinary action, and Gracia Mendes became the prime mover of the plan. After several meetings with family members, a call was issued for a complete boycott of the harbor of Ancona. The boycott was to last for eight months, after which time the results were to be assessed and new measures contemplated. The appeal for the boycott was sent to the entire Marrano Diaspora, which included the large community of Salonika, as well as those in Italy and the Netherlands. The plan found enthusiastic approval in the Marrano group associated with the Mendes family and in every community reached by the message. Suleiman himself took a personal and official interest in its execution. In fact, through a special emissary, a French Christian nobleman, Suleiman sent a letter to the pope asking for protection for those he designated "his" Jewish subjects. Although the document reads as though it were motivated by economics rather than human compassion, it is one of the rare examples of the intervention by an important ruler on behalf of his Jewish citizens:

... When you shall have received my Divine and Imperial Seal, which will be presented to you, you must know that certain persons of the race of the Jews have informed my Elevated and Sublime Porte that, whereas certain subjects and tributaries of Ours have gone to your territories to traffic and especially to Ancona, their goods and property have been seized on your instructions. This is in particular to the prejudice of Our Treasury, to the amount of four hundred thousand ducats, over and above the damage done to our subjects, who have been ruined and cannot pay their obligations to Our said Treasury, on account of the customs duties and commerce of Our Ports which they had in their hands.

The papal response was polite and noncommittal. By the time it was received in Constantinople, most of the prisoners had already been burned at the stake and their property confiscated. The sultan had done more than his duty. It was now up to the Jews to avenge their dead. The results of their efforts could soon be felt. Countless business ventures in Ancona went bankrupt, and the once busy harbor was almost empty. Merchandise, originally designated for Ancona, went to Pessaro in the north, or to other ports.

Though at first the boycott seemed effective, it failed in the end. It failed not because of the determination of the pope, but because those Italian Jews who were not Marranos felt threatened themselves by the boycott. Not only were they afraid that their temporarily peaceful existence in Italy would be jeopardized, they feared commercial reprisals as well. Cowardice—shared and expressed by the Sephardic rabbis of Italy—and a lack of historic perspective rendered the boycott ineffective. The Marranos of Ancona were dead or had fled the city. The house of Mendes closed the doors of its offices in the harbor city. No ship of the famous bank ever made port in Ancona again—but others did. The rabbis of Ancona pleaded on behalf of the remaining Jewish (non-Marrano) community, which was bound to suffer from the boycott. The Turkish rabbis wavered in their support of Doña Gracia. After a few months the boycott had to be called off.

Both in the planning stage and its stipulated goals, the Ancona affair was the antithesis of what is sometimes considered the traditional Jewish resignation to their fate as a persecuted minority. Had it succeeded, it might have served as a model for future generations. But the design came from the Jewish aristocrats whose great wealth and political power made them impervious to reprisals or persecutions. The majority of the Jews still lived with memories of past persecutions which were too powerful for them to forget, and with the actual threat of future tortures if they dared to take action against the authorities. It was not until the establishment of the State of Israel that Jews really felt that they had mastery over their fate. Until then Jews, with some notable exceptions like that of the defenders of the Warsaw ghetto, continued to meet their fate stoically and with the kind of resignation that met the pleas of Joseph Nasi and Doña Gracia.

During the years following the Ancona affair, Joseph Nasi became increasingly involved in Suleiman's family. Although it is not known what role Joseph Nasi played in the royal family's tragedies, there are some who claim that he had financed Selim, the sultan's son, in a struggle for power in which he eliminated his brothers. There is little proof of this charge. What is known is that Joseph Nasi was eager to maintain a close relationship with the royal court.

It was imperative for him to cultivate the successor to Suleiman, who was now in his late sixties. It is reported that when Selim served as governor of a province in Asia Minor, Nasi undertook the long and arduous journey to bring him "precious vestments, thoroughbred horses and diamond-encrusted weapons," with the acclamation: "It is your destiny, my prince, to succeed your father to the throne."

Selim, in turn, had persuaded his father to grant Nasi possession of the region around the Lake of Tiberias in Palestine. He was undoubtedly familiar with another of Joseph Nasi's plans: to settle fellow Marranos in the Holy Land. This premature Zionist notion is further testimony to Joseph Nasi's imaginative view of Jewish history. Suleiman had no special interest in Palestine so long as the Muslim shrines of Jerusalem were not endangered, and he was eager to please the house of Mendes, which had done him so many favors. He deeded to Nasi not only the ruins of Tiberias but seven of the neighboring villages. Nasi appointed Rabbi Joseph ben Ardut as his agent in charge of rebuilding the walls of the city. Ben Ardut arrived in Tiberias with an order from the sultan that "All laborers and builders in the seven villages must report for the rebuilding of Tiberias. He who does not appear will be punished."

Since Tiberias had once been a great city, there was an abundance of building stone, and for mixing the mortar, the workers had all the sand surrounding the Sea of Galilee. As the work began, a leader of one of the villages warned the Arab workers that if they continued to build the city their "religion would be destroyed." This had been prophesied, according to the seer, in an old book. The workers promptly stopped the building. Joseph ben Ardut went immediately to the pasha of Damascus and complained that an order of the sultan had been disobeyed. The terrified pasha had the two leaders of the Arab workers arrested and executed. The strike was broken and the building was concluded. According to Joseph Ha-Kohen, a contemporary of Nasi who included the whole story in his book *Vale of Tears*, the circumference of Tiberias was fifteen hundred cubits when the work was finished in late November 1564.

The next step was the planting of hundreds of mulberry trees, for Nasi had developed a detailed plan for the prospective settlers of Tiberias. They were to raise silkworms and establish an industry which would rival that of the city of Venice. Thus, in addition to its Zionist goal, the settlement of Tiberias would discomfit that city so hated by the Mendes family.

Joseph Nasi's plan for the Holy Land was remarkable because it had all the features of twentieth-century social planning: freedom, security and a self-sufficient, prosperous economy to support the people. But in 1564 Joseph Nasi was just a visionary. The Marranos did not respond. They evidently preferred urban life, however dangerous or tenuous, to life in isolated Tiberias. The city reverted to ruins; the houses which had been erected remained empty. The mulberry trees were never cultivated, and in time, withered and died.

Joseph Nasi had understood that the plight of the Marranos of Ancona and the repeated exile of his people into other parts of the world were a warning that the Jews needed a homeland of their own. It was not until three hundred years later that Theodor Herzl translated the same urgency that Joseph Nasi had felt into the reality of modern Zionism.

Suleiman the Magnificent, who had ruled the Ottoman Empire for forty years and had made it into the most powerful political entity of the sixteenth century, died in 1566. His son Selim, as expected, succeeded him, Joseph Nasi at his side. Selim II had inherited the throne but, unfortunately, none of the greatness of his father. He is remembered in the history of Turkey as Selim the Drunk and reigned for only eight years. Nothing much was accomplished during his reign and a large part of his failure was due to a strange Marranic conflict. His two advisers were his grand vizier and Joseph Nasi. When the grand vizier counseled close relationship with Venice, Joseph Nasi advised against it. It had become a rule for him that no Marrano could make peace with Venice. So an important alliance which could have benefited the empire was not consummated.

As soon as Selim ascended the throne he bestowed upon his friend Nasi the title of Duke of Naxos and the Aegean Islands. It was a high honor for a non-Muslim to actually have governing power over the islands, but Joseph Nasi deputized a Christian of Jewish descent to serve as governor.

After Selim's death Nasi retired from public life to devote himself mainly to furthering Jewish scholarship. He attracted Jewish thinkers to Constantinople, established a Hebrew printing press in Belvedere, and remained to the end of his life the great powerful protector of the Marranos. He died in 1579 in his early seventies.

While most Marranos were satisfied to find a haven of refuge, to return to Judaism and live in peace, Joseph Nasi and the house of Mendes, one of the richest and noblest of the Marrano families, never forgot that they were part of a large brotherhood of Marranos, and they never forgot those who had caused the Marranos pain.

Chapter Six

In 1908 Carlos I, the extravagant and licentious king of Portugal, was assassinated in the street. His son Manuel II, who succeeded him, turned out to be an equally unenlightened monarch. In October 1910 the people forced Manuel to abdicate and to flee to England. The coup, in the end, proved abortive. By 1912, following the failure of a general strike, the entire country, from Lisbon to the rural areas, was caught up in the hope for new freedom.

The provinces were even more impatient for revolution than the capital. In August 1910, two months before the abdication, Oporto, the "Capital of the North" and Lisbon's ancient rival, provided the catalyst for the revolution. The people of Oporto prided themselves on their activism. There was an old saying: "Coimbra sings, Braga prays, Lisbon shows off, but Oporto works and acts." On that August day the republican leaders and their followers assembled in Oporto's square. Longshoremen from the famous port mingled with the radical intellectuals. They had gathered to witness a symbolic act to serve notice to the country and the world that the time for revolution had come.

The main actor in this performance was a young man long known to the literati and intellectuals of Oporto as a person of fervor and daring. His name was Arturo Carlos de Barros Basto. While the crowd cheered, Basto climbed to the roof of the town hall and replaced the royal flag with the banner of the revolution. This gesture symbolized the political mood of Oporto, and it turned out to be an important impetus for the abdication of the king. Basto became a patriotic hero.

Barros Basto is important to us not because of his heroic political act, but because he was destined to discover the hiding places of Portugal's more than fifteen thousand Marranos. We are indebted to him for much of our information about these crypto-Jews. At the time of the flag raising on the roof they were still living in almost total obscurity, and it was not generally known that Basto himself was a descendant of Jews.

Basto was born in Amaranta on the river Tamaga but grew up in Oporto in the home of his grandfather, who, in accordance with Marrano tradition, imparted the secret of his Jewish heritage to Basto on his thirteenth birthday. He was not taught more than the faint recollections which had been handed down through the generations of his family, but some passionate stirrings must have been awakened in him. From his earliest youth Basto apparently harbored a desire to return to the religion of his Jewish ancestors. His grandfather himself does not seem to have considered such an idea; he lived like all the other Marranos of Oporto, openly a Catholic, privately, and largely in his memories, a Jew. For him it was enough to have carried out his family duty by telling his grandson the secret of his Jewish heritage.

After the usual education of children of the middle class, Basto chose a military career. During World War I, when Portugal sided with the Allies, he fought "with distinction" and returned to his homeland a hero. He was appointed press censor and director of military prisons. His office was located in an ancient building which had once been a synagogue. For the rest of Basto's life he considered this curious coincidence a sign of the validity of his secret wish to convert to Judaism.

Since the Jewish community of Oporto was so small that it had neither rabbi nor synagogue—the occasional Sabbath services were held in a private home—Barros Basto decided to go to Lisbon to make his public declaration during services in the small but dignified synagogue there. He sat quietly in his pew, a young man wearing the uniform of an officer, decorated with the British and Portuguese medals of valor which he had received during the war. To the worshipers, he was, of course, a stranger. They looked at him with curiosity but asked no questions. The prayer book lay open before him but he did not know Hebrew and had to follow the prayers in the Portuguese translation. Basto seems to have learned the order of the service, however, and he waited for the dramatic moment he had chosen, the most important part of the Sabbath service, the reading from the Torah—the sacred scroll which contains the five books of Moses.

The scrolls are considered the most precious possession of any congregation. They are dressed in velvet mantles, covered with silver ornaments and kept in the ark, hidden from the congregation behind lavishly ornamented curtains. The moment when the ark is opened with the singing of an ancient prayer is of great significance to Jews. The scroll is taken out and the rabbi, who kisses the Torah which he holds in his arms, turns to the congregation and says the prayer which admonishes the Jews to adhere to the ancient faith: "Hear O Israel, the Lord our God is One." In order to emphasize the singleness of God, the word "One" is spoken with great fervor and is drawn out so that no breath is left in the rabbi's body to utter another word.

This was the moment which Barros Basto had waited for. He left his seat, a soldier in uniform, acting as though he were attacking an enemy position. He stormed the pulpit, seized the scroll, kissed it, and with great passion pronounced the only Hebrew he knew, *"Shema Yisrael"*— Hear O Israel. He quickly added, in Portuguese, "Your God, who is One, is my God. From the world of the Trinity I am returning to the kingdom of one God, the God of Israel, the creator of the world. I am one of your people. Your people is my people. I am a Marrano. I wish to be accepted into the Jewish brotherhood."

They asked him to return to his seat. The rabbi agreed to meet him after the service, which, one can imagine, was concluded in some haste. Still, no member of the congregation spoke to Basto. After the service the rabbi and the elders of the synagogue received him. He told them about his grandfather, about his Marranic background, his new belief, his deep conviction which urged him to return to Judaism. He asked for admission into the Jewish community and offered to submit to circumcision. But the reaction of the leaders of the congregation was disheartening. They rejected his plea.

Basto did not realize that he was facing one of the most frightened and timid Jewish communities in the world. The Jews of Portugal had their own haunting memories. Since the fifteenth century there had been no national community in Portugal. The persecutions under King Manuel I (son-in-law of Ferdinand and Isabella) had forced thousands of Jews into baptism. His royal decree in 1497, declaring that all the remaining Jews were slaves, was followed by a slaughter which in brutality rivals any persecution in Jewish history. Not until the middle of the nineteenth century did a handful of Jews return to Portugal. At first they were not even allowed to have a synagogue. When the revolution of 1910 granted them the same religious freedoms which it briefly gave to other Portuguese citizens, the Jews remained timid. No Jew had dared to participate in the political struggle in which Basto had been so active, for they considered themselves tolerated settlers rather than fully accepted citizens.

By 1918, when Basto appeared in the synagogue, times had again become difficult for everyone. The Catholic Church had been defeated and humiliated by the revolution of 1910, which had forced it to denounce celibacy and permit its priests to marry. The Church was not likely to forget those experiences now that it had regained its old power. For a Jewish community, ill at ease and fearful of a repetition of persecutions, the conversion of Barros Basto, a Roman Catholic, might seriously threaten their existence. The young man left the synagogue, but he was by no means prepared to give up his plans. If he could not be converted in Portugal, he would turn to another country.

Basto devoted the next two years to the study of Hebrew and Jewish history. When he had mastered both, he again decided that he was ready for conversion and applied to the Sephardic chief rabbi of Morocco. The circumcision and conversion took place in 1920 in Tangiers, one of the oldest

North African Jewish communities which, at that time, had a Jewish population of ten thousand. According to Jewish custom, every male convert receives the name of Abraham in honor of Abraham, the first Jew. Thus, Basto was named Abraham ben Rosh.

He returned to Portugal a Jew. But in addition to all the obligations which a pious Jew is called upon to assume, Basto had decided to take on a Jewish career. He would bring Judaism to the secret Jews of Portugal. He became a Jewish missionary to his Marrano brothers.

The Portuguese Marranos were assumed to be a forgotten tribe. Few people admitted knowing of their existence. But when Basto proclaimed publicly that he wanted to set out, like Joseph in the Bible, to "find his brothers," he discovered that it was actually common knowledge that most of the Marranos lived in the mountainous region of Portugal known as the Beira Baixa.

The Beira Baixa is the poorest part of the country. The winters are glacial, the summers unbearably hot. The poor crops have to struggle against the terrible climate and the rocky soil. The neo-Christians had probably moved to this inhospitable region during the bloody years of persecution because they felt safer there than in the large towns, and in this barren isolation, protected from the influence of the large cities, old customs could more readily be preserved. The Marranos had gone to the mountains during the fifteenth century; a decade after World War I, Barros Basto found them still living fifteenth-century lives in Belmonte, in Fundão, in Covilhã, and in many other little villages. They were pious, primitive, superstitious peasants or small businessmen. All of them were ostensibly sons and daughters of the Church. They crossed themselves when they passed a crucifix or a statue of a saint; they went to village churches to receive absolution and joined the Christian villagers in prayer; in every room of their houses there were the statues of those saints that protected their crops and their family lives.

But they were a different sort of Catholic. They were conscious of the fact that in spite of their Catholic piety they were *judeu*—hidden Jews. They ate the same simple food as their neighbors, but, if possible, they did not eat pork. On the Sabbath or a Jewish holiday they did not eat meat at all. According to contemporary accounts, even a hundred years before Basto rediscovered the people, pork was never eaten. By 1920 the prohibition had been relaxed.

Every evening after the church bells had tolled for the last time, the Jews of Beira Baixa rose and said: "O God, give us this hour of grace. Cause our suffering to end and permit us to see our victory with our own eyes. Let our teachings be spread here and on the holy mountain of Jerusalem." This is a Marrano—a Jewish—prayer. But the hidden Jews of the mountains of Portugal don't know of the existence of today's Jerusalem. When they pray, they mean only the ancient city of the Great Temple of Solomon. They have no idea what contemporary Judaism means. To them Judaism is a strange rite practiced only clandestinely. Open Jewish services and free Jewish existence, as we know it, is not authentic Judaism to them. And the Jewish customs that they observe are often only half-understood distortions of Judaism as it really exists.

One of the centers of Portuguese Marranism that Basto uncovered is Monsanto, a village rich in Portuguese history and customs. However, the Marranos of Monsanto have their own ancient memories, and their customs are also very old. When a Marrano in Monsanto is near death, no priest is permitted to be present at the deathbed. When the Marrano dies, nine men of the community arrive so that with the dead man they form a *minyan*, the Jewish quorum for prayer. They wrap the corpse in a white shroud and say to him: "You will come to the valley of Jehosaphat where our dead are judged. There Satan will come to you and he will ask you, 'What is your faith?' and you will respond in these words: 'All my life I have been a Hebrew, and if I have not done everything that God demanded of me, it is only because in my ignorance, I did not know what to do.' "

This answer is reminiscent of an interesting document found among the records of the Mexican Inquisition in the Francisco Rivas Library in Mexico City. It reads: "This is the case of Juan Méndez, age twenty-three, not circumcised, son of the gatekeeper of the church, who admitted that because of the Jewish blood of his grandmother he has a certain tendency to doubt the validity of the Christian faith. During the ecclesiastical interrogation the young man said this sentence: 'If I knew that the Law of Moses really existed, I should without any doubt adhere to it.' " There is hardly a better definition of the Marranic way of life which Basto found in Monsanto and the other villages he visited. It is a life of faint memory, based on vague tradition rather than certain knowledge.

Barros Basto continued for many years on his missionary journey. Wherever he could find Marranos, whether in the poor and primitive villages or in the homes of the rich and sophisticated citizens of the larger cities, he tried to convince them to return to their ancient religion. He gained a public reputation as a fervent proselytizer, intolerant and totally absorbed in his cause, but to the Marranos he was the "Master."

The master did not travel alone. Two physicians whom he had converted in Oporto became the official circumcisers. The group traveled by rail, car or mule, a strange twentieth-century missionary caravan, something that has no parallel in all of Jewish history.

I arrived in Braganza [capital of Trás-os-Montes province] on Sunday evening, October 16, 1927 [Basto wrote]. Several crypto-Jews awaited me at the station. There were greetings and small talk. Most of these people were of the opinion that nothing could be done, as the majority of the Marrano families were still afraid to avow their faith publicly. But I decided to approach several families on Monday morning. I put on my uniform and presented myself, accompanied by several gentlemen known in the community as Jews. We told the servants who received us to inform their masters that a Jewish officer from Oporto wished to speak with them. We succeeded to a certain extent. The elderly women who had joined us wept with joy mixed with fear. During the following day we circumcised five men.

The movement spread. Basto found some villages where the majority of the inhabitants was crypto-Jews. In the ancient city of Moncorvo, which had once been a Portuguese center of Jewish learning, he found a hundred clandestine Jews. In Mogadouro and in Vilharno, not far from Braganza, practically all the inhabitants were Marranos. Basto conducted services in both towns, and they were attended by the strangest people, some of whom had never been known to be Marranos. Since no one knew Hebrew, all services were conducted in Portuguese. The prayer book had been prepared by Basto in advance of his excursions.

In Braganza most of the rich Marranos were afraid to come, but some did. A general and a major, both of an old family of landed gentry, attended and spoke—for the first time in many generations—of their Marranic tradition, reporting that according to family custom, their women did not usually attend church services. However, on those occasions when they did, they would meet with other crypto-Jews after the services, and in a back room, away from the windows, they would conduct a special service for Marrano women. There they would say the prayer of Esther, whom they considered to have been the first Jewish Marrano. In the story which is the basis of the Jewish holiday of Purim, Esther was married to the king of Persia, who did not know that she was Jewish. When the king's minister plotted to kill all the Jews, Esther revealed herself to the king as a Jew and thereby saved her people. So, like the Marranos, Esther had worshiped a strange god and had had to conceal her Jewish origins.

The Marrano women of Braganza prayed in the words of Queen Esther: "O my Lord, thou art our king. Help me, a desolate woman, who has no helper but thee; for my danger is in thy hand. Since my youth I have heard in the tribe of my family that thou, O God, tookest Israel from among all people and our fathers from all their predecessors for a perpetual inheritance, and thou hast performed whatsoever thou didst promise them. And now we have sinned before thee. Therefore thou hast given us into the hands of our enemies because we have worshiped their gods. O Lord, thou art righteous."

"Santa Esther" became the Jewish Marranic counterpart of Santa Maria. Since they had learned for centuries to think in terms of the Catholic Church, turning the Jewish woman, Esther, into a saint was a natural transformation. For them the parallel between their fate and that of Esther was too apparent to be overlooked. And since Esther's story ends with Israel's redemption, the worship was also comforting and hopeful. They knelt before the Catholic madonna, but their thoughts were with Esther, the Jewish woman who had worshiped the gods of Persia. The Marranos of Braganza lived the uneasy lives of *conversòs*, haunted by their ancestors' betrayal of Judaism and tormented by their own inability to leave the Church and openly worship the god of Santa Esther.

For Barros Basta each meeting with these clandestine Portuguese Jews was an encounter with his brethren. He had drawn singular consequences from the discovery that he was a Marrano. He had done more than just return to Judaism; he was determined to help his fellow Marranos find their peace as Jews as he had done. But he was not ultimately successful. In spite of the fact that congregations of returned Marranos were founded and even synagogues built through his efforts, they did not survive him. He founded a magazine, written and published for the Marranos who had found their way back to Judaism. It bore the proud name of *Halapid*, the Torch. A few copies can still be found in some libraries, a touching but very small monument to the passion of the man who patiently taught Judaism to adults as if he were teaching children. But like the congregations, the magazine did not last. It was Basto's personal tragedy that he did not raise a son or find a successor who could have continued his work. After his death in 1961 little was left of his revolutionary movement. Like the political cause that he had helped to lead in 1910, his personal quest had failed.

. . . .

The other "explorer" who discovered the Portuguese Marranos was Samuel Schwarz, a Jewish mining engineer from Poland who, in 1915, was invited by the Portuguese government to survey the geological conditions of the country. Two years later he found himself in Belmonte, an almost inaccessible spot in the north of Portugal, not far from the Spanish border. It was here that he discovered the Marranos. His fascinating experiences are described in his book *The Neo-Christians of Portugal in the Twentieth Century*, published in 1925 at the height of Barros Basto's missionary work. To Schwarz the discovery, which he reported with so much enthusiasm and in such great detail, was merely a curious footnote to Jewish history as he knew it. Unlike Basto, he had no plans for the Marranos. He collected as much material about them as he could and reported on what he found, but it never entered his mind to convert them to Judaism. He was a deeply committed Jew, perhaps uncommonly interested in Jewish history, but he was essentially a scientist reporting an unusual species. If he and Basto ever met, there is no record of their encounter.

Adonai, the Hebrew name for God, remains the only Hebrew word remembered by the Portuguese Marranos, and it was this word that actually led to Schwarz's discovery of the mountain "Jews" in Belmonte. Schwarz knew that Belmonte had once been the seat of a famous Jewish community with a thirteenth-century synagogue which had been taken over by the Church, but he did not think that there were any Jews still living in the city. So he was surprised when he was warned by a merchant delivering fuel to him not to buy anything from his competitor across the street because "his name is Baltazar Pereira de Sousa and he is a Jew." The de Sousas had been faithful Christians for centuries, so it intrigued Schwarz that they were still considered Jews, and that the word "Jew" was spoken by the rival merchant with the same sort of contempt that anti-Semitic Poles used for Jewish competitors in his hometown. He decided to go to see this "Jew."

It took some persuading, but after a time the merchant admitted to Schwarz and his companions that he was, indeed, a secret Jew. However, he added, he was currently something of an outcast among his own people because he had married a Christian woman, "which is not done among our people." Fascinated, Schwarz asked the man to introduce him to the other hidden Jews of Belmonte. Perhaps because the merchant was in disfavor or simply because the Belmonte Marranos believed that Jews no longer existed, they refused to believe Schwarz when he said he was a Jew. The men in particular were skeptical. But one of the women said, "Since you pretend to know Jewish prayers different from ours, recite them to us in Hebrew, since you claim that Hebrew is the language of the Jews." Schwarz pointed out to them that they did not understand Hebrew, but the women insisted, and so Schwarz and his friends began to recite the most familiar, most often spoken Hebrew prayers. Schwarz describes the event in his book:

It was a delightful summer afternoon. A gentle breeze filled the air. From afar we could see the beauty of Serra de Estrela which the rays of the sun filled with such glorious light, reminding us of the Biblical description of Mount Sinai. Then suddenly something utterly unforeseen happened. One of my friends decided to recite the most sublime of Jewish prayers, said daily by every Jew, the prayer that proclaims the Oneness of our God. "Hear O Israel, the Lord our God is One." This is the prayer which the Jews, prisoners of the Inquisition, must have pronounced and often screamed in the hour of their despair. My friends said in Hebrew: *"Shema Yisrael, Adonai Elohenu, Adonai Echad."*

When he said the word Adonai, the women, as though in ecstasy, covered their eyes with their hands, and one of them, an old woman, recited a prayer in Portuguese saying in an authoritative voice as the *sacerdotisa,* the one who leads in prayers and knows them all: "He is really a Jew, for he knows how to pronounce properly the name of our Lord Adonai."

In Belmonte it is the mothers who pass on to their daughters on their eleventh birthday the secret of their Jewish heritage. The little girls are told that Judaism is a religion to be practiced in secret and that they are to forget what the priest taught them. The mothers then teach their daughters the special Marrano prayers. The first to be learned is the prayer of forgiveness: "Forgive me, Adonai. I did not know your law, but now that I know it I shall keep it." There is also a special Marrano version of the Lord's Prayer, the Pater Noster: "O Lord, thou who art in heaven because of thy grace, thou permittest the sinners to call you Pater Noster, our Father. But I, Adonai, I cannot pray as they do, for I know thou alone art in heaven. Look down from heaven on our misery and help us, O Lord, in thy goodness and from all our sins redeem us. Give us, O Adonai, zeal and fervor to serve thee, and save us in this world from their evil doing." When the Marranos of Belmonte enter the church, dip their hands into the holy water and make the sign of the cross, they seem to be like all the other Catholic members of the congregation. But, quietly, they say, "I swear and confirm that this is but wood and stone, and nobody is the Lord but thee."

Schwarz had arrived in Belmonte in the spring. Walking through the village, he noticed a group of people who were baking small unleavened cakes. The villagers had not eaten any bread for three days before the unleavened cakes were distributed, and when he spoke to them and learned this, Schwarz realized that he was witnessing a Marrano version of Passover. They called it the time of Pasqua. In the past, in order to escape the watchful eyes of the Inquisition, the Marranos would start the holiday three days earlier than known Jews did. These villagers had long forgotten the word "matzot," the Hebrew name for unleavened bread. They call it *pāo santo*, holy bread, and in accordance with a Jewish custom that can be traced back to the days of the ancient Temple in Jerusalem, the women throw the first part of the dough into the fire.

One family is designated for the special honor of baking the *pāo santo*. The whole Marrano community gathers in this family's home, which is thoroughly cleaned as, traditionally, all Jewish homes are cleaned for the holiday. The floors are covered with white linen. Like certain Orthodox Jews throughout the world, the women wear white dresses, the men cover themselves in white garments resembling the shrouds in which they will be buried.

Special china is used during the Marrano Passover, as it is in Jewish homes. The flour is put into special bowls and special prayers are said. While the bread is baking, everybody kneels. It should be noted that kneeling is a gesture almost unknown among Jews, except in the symbolic kneeling of the rabbi during the High Holy Days. When the unleavened bread is ready, the people rise, kiss one another, and each family takes home its share of the holy bread wrapped in white cloth. There is also a special Passover wine. It is prepared during the autumn months and stored in barrels which no one is permitted to touch. The wine is pure, and unlike the ordinary wine the people drink during the year, does not contain any spices.

No Marrano in Belmonte works during the week of Passover. The villagers meet three times a day for prayer, the traditional timetable for daily prayer of the pious Jew. On one of the days they gather for a Passover picnic somewhere in the mountains, praying and singing and dancing. The dance is stately, like the ritual dances of Africa; the song is unique and distinctive, and is sung only during this one week in the mountains of Portugal. Then the people go to a river, and waving olive branches, recite the "water prayers." The olive branches may be a recollection of the Jewish harvest festival of Sukkoth, in which the branches of three plants are used and during which, in Jewish antiquity, a feast of water pouring was performed. In Belmonte the Marranos sing while waving the olive branches: "There comes Moses with his raised switch to beat the sea." They beat the surface of the river hoping it may part in a repetition of the miraculous parting of the Red Sea. The olive branches used in the ceremony are kept throughout the year, and in the following spring they are used to light the oven in which the *pão santo* will be baked.

The Sabbath is also observed in a special way. On Friday afternoon the woman of the house prepares the "Candle of the Lord," a wick of fresh linen dipped in pure olive oil. These wicks have seven threads, and they are prepared by people specially trained to say certain prayers continuously until the wick is properly woven. The wick is then placed in a jar as it was during the Inquisition when the Marranos took great care not to betray their Jewishness. (This braided wick may be a faint memory of the candle used by

Jews in the ceremony of *Havdallah,* which bids farewell to
the Sabbath at the end of the day when three stars have appeared in the sky. According to authentic Jewish custom, it
is a candle made of seven strands of wax braided together.)
In Belmonte the Sabbath meal begins with a prayer, as
does Friday night in Jewish homes all over the world. In
Hebrew the Sabbath prayer is called *Kiddush.* But the
Marranos remember only a distortion of the sound of the
Hebrew word, and they call their prayer *Idus.* Of course,
to make sure no pork is eaten, no meat is served on the
Sabbath.

The Sabbath is not merely ritually observed, but as in any
Orthodox Jewish community, affects ordinary commercial
transactions. Samuel Schwarz reported a scene he observed
on a Friday afternoon in 1922 in Belmonte. A Marrano
merchant was sitting at a hotel table conversing with a
prospective customer who was eager to buy some articles
not obtainable in any other stores. It was late in the afternoon, and while they were still discussing the price, night
fell. The Marrano excused himself and went home. The
next day the customer, eager to finalize the deal, offered the
Marrano a higher price than that proposed on Friday. The
Marrano, however, refused to deal with him on the Sabbath
and asked him to return after sunset. When the man came
to see him again, he was prepared to pay the price he had
suggested earlier in the day, but the Marrano refused. He
would take only the price agreed to on Friday because he
did not want to profit from a business deal contracted on
the Sabbath.

When the Marranos of Belmonte rise in the morning they
say in medieval Portuguese, the language they and their
ancestors had spoken before King Manuel I forced them to

become Catholics: "May the Lord Adonai keep me from my enemies, those who wish me ill and those who talk badly about me; the injustices of the Inquisition and the irons of the king, of all that is bad. May the Lord of Israel save me. Amen, O Lord Adonai, to heaven He goes and in heaven He arrives."

For these hidden Jews there might as well still be an Inquisition. They speak of King Manuel I in their prayers as if he were still alive. They still live in fear of an institution which has long been abandoned and of a king who died in 1521.

In the evening they lie in their beds and say: "I now lie down and am as always in thy power, O Adonai. Great are thy mercies, for we must make our devotions. Praised be Adonai when we lie down and praised be Adonai when we get up. In thy power are the souls of the dead, in thy power are the souls of the living. To thee, O Lord Adonai, I commend my soul and all that thou hast given me and may give me in the future."

They are still afraid that their Judaic past might be discovered. On the way to the fields or their shops they say: "Bless me, O Lord Adonai, go with me forever, grant me thy grace and thy shelter, thy goodness and thy love. Please do me the great favor that nobody should betray me, that only the angels of the highest Lord Adonai accompany me forever." They say: "Adonai is the Lord. He is my shelter and my castle. May I not fear the dread of the night nor the spies who spy in the afternoon or the great slaughter of the darkness."

This anxiety has developed into a curious collective paranoia. The fear of something that existed hundreds of years ago, transmitted from one generation to the next, has created something like a congenital neurosis, so that in the twentieth century the Marranos of Belmonte are still afraid. The timetable of their terrible, unshakable memories is very old: 1391, the slaughter of Seville; 1405, the bloodbath of Toledo; 1492, the expulsion from Spain; 1497, the massacre of Lisbon. Yet, the memories of all of these events are still very much alive in the mountains of Portugal.

The discovery of the Portuguese Marranos by Barros Basto and Samuel Schwarz was followed a few years later by the revelation that a whole community of Marranos existed on the Balearic Islands. Here the secret Jews are called *chuetas,* which means "swine," and may refer to the pots of steaming, cooking pork that they traditionally kept in front of their doorsteps to prove to the world that they were pork eaters and therefore not Jews.

Shortly before Hitler's ascent to power, Ezriel Carlebach, a German Jewish journalist descended from an old Orthodox rabbinical family, published his book entitled *Exotic Jews.* In it he described his journey to the prosperous Jews of the island of Majorca. (He evidently did not know that there were also eight *chueta* families, recognized as former Jews, on the much smaller island of Ibiza.) Ezriel Carlebach knew he would find *chuetas* in Palma de Majorca, for their existence had been common knowledge for a long time. But no Jewish historian or folklorist had bothered to visit them before Carlebach did in 1930.

He was directed to the "Jewish Quarter," which consisted of thirty houses, twenty of them with jewelry stores on the first floor. Some of the houses were simple, others very attractive. In the shop windows there were statues of saints, many different versions of Mary, crucifixes, baptismal fonts, Christian silver amulets of all sorts, and photographs of the pope. When Carlebach saw these exhibits of Christian religious artifacts, he was certain that he had been misdirected. This could not be the "Jewish Quarter," and these stores could not have anything to do with the "Jewish merchants" of whom he had been told. He started to leave the street, to try and find more reliable information about the *chuetas*. As he walked toward the arch which formed the entrance to the quarter, he saw a Majorcan spitting with much gusto and contempt at the street and muttering something about the "cursed *judíos*." Then he knew that he had come to the right place. The crosses that he had seen in the showcases were part of the schizophrenic life of the Majorcan *chuetas*. To Carlebach they became "the crosses of Jewish fate."

Carlebach went back into the narrow street, part of a medieval town which was now only a mecca for tourists and sightseers, though it had once been an important Spanish outpost. He was determined to find out whether anything was left of the Jewish memory which, it seemed to him, haunted the place, so he went into one of the stores. The "Jewish" silversmiths bending over their workbenches on a silver statue of the madonna were pious Catholics. And not merely pious in the ordinary sense, but obsessed with it.

I looked at the eyes of the man who moved slowly toward the counter. His eyes were sad. I was under the impression, probably utterly unfounded, that he looked at me somehow knowingly. First we gazed at each other without speaking a word. Then he inquired simply what I was looking for. I said, "A ring."

"A ring," he said with some regret, "but you can have rings everywhere. I specialize in holy articles, beautiful madonnas, a crucifix studded with precious stones. A ring is an ordinary thing. The statue of a saint will help you to live piously." But I insisted that all I wanted was a ring. To be sure, I could get rings in any other store, but the ring I wanted to buy was not an ordinary ring. I was looking for one with a special inscription. "What kind of inscription?" he asked. Speaking slowly, I looked at him intensely. "A ring with the word 'Zion' or 'Adonai.'" I had hoped to discover some reaction in his eyes, a gleam, some excitement, a flushed face. Nothing. He looked at the shelves, opened some glass cases. Two women who had been in the store as I came in tried to help him. "Too bad," he said, and the women nodded in agreement, "but I do not have any such thing. As I told you, I specialize in crucifixes and other holy articles. I am sorry." They looked at each other, shrugging their shoulders again, looking at each other as though they had found a rather strange customer. I glanced at them once more and then left.

But Carlebach did not give up. Sometime later he returned to the store. This time he no longer pretended to be a customer. He had decided to let the storekeeper know that he had come to inquire about the Marranos. As proof, he had brought some issues of Barros Basto's magazine *Halapid*, which he showed to the old man. The silversmith showed no interest in them, nor did he seem to recognize a picture of Basto of whom he would have heard if he were, indeed, a Marrano. Finally, Carlebach showed him a personal letter which Basto had written to him. The silversmith looked at the picture and then at the letter, but he returned them with a strange, shy smile. Carlebach began to think that the man really did not know anything about the Marranos. But he couldn't believe it.

"I probably had expected too much," he wrote. "People here who for hundreds of years had learned and practiced the art of silence were not going to reveal their secrets to a complete stranger. I had acted with too much haste. I had to learn to be patient."

It was in this mood that he strolled in the streets of the old city, passing many churches and medieval houses until he came to a Dominican monastery. Suddenly something which he seemed to have forgotten occurred to him. He walked into the monastery, through the dark halls, into the cloister. The walls were covered with hangings and pictures. He stood in front of one of them. It looked as though it had been painted with blood.

And then he remembered that in the early seventeenth century a few *chueta* families who had lived the life of deceit and pretense decided to end it all and flee from an island which had denied them acceptance because their ancestors had been forced to convert in the fifteenth century. One night they packed up and escaped to the harbor where they boarded a little boat. It was hardly seaworthy. The fifty-six Marranos, who had decided to join their Jewish brothers in Italy, to return to Judaism and to be free again, sat tightly together. Before they started on their daring journey, they joined hands and together recited the prayer of *Kol Nidre*, which is said on the eve of the Day of Atonement. It had special reference to Marrano existence, and some scholars think it may even have been written for Marranos. "All the oaths that we swore and all the promises that we made, may they all be declared as null and void as though they had had never been made. Pardon us, O Lord, and forgive our sins!"

They left the harbor . . . but a few hours later a storm broke the mast and they were back in Palma. A quickly gathering mob watched the boat and its desperate crew in jubilant expectation of what they knew would happen when the boat landed. As soon as it reached the shore, the crowd threw itself on these helpless men, women and children whose families had lived on the island for generations. No trial was needed. For *chuetas* to leave the island without permission was a capital crime, punishable by death. All of them were burned on a pyre which had speedily been built in the court of the monastery. The picture in the cloisters depicted the gruesome scene. Below the picture was a cross. It was made from the bones of one of the *judíos*.

Perhaps Carlebach had been drawn to the monastery because it was the evening of the Day of Atonement. Soon the *Kol Nidre* prayer, which in his mind was associated with the Marranos, would be chanted in synagogues all over the world. But there was no synagogue in Palma. Since for the first time in his life he would not be attending a service on this holy night, he decided that he would commemorate the holiday in a daring new way, among the *chuetas* of Majorca. It was already dark. In the streets the people were on their way home, and priests in long black robes walked into the church to celebrate the mass.

Carlebach was in a somber mood. He went back to the place where he had met defeat twice before. The shop was situated on the same street where the *conversos* had lived for centuries, the Calle de Sayel. He took along the Portuguese prayer book of the Marranos which Barros Basto had published in Oporto. He was sure the *chuetas* would understand it, although their language was, of course, Spanish. He walked once more into the store. "I placed the prayerbook on the table right in front of the three *chuetas*, the man and the two women. And then I said quietly but defiantly, 'I am staying here with you and I shall read with you from the prayer book which contains the prayers of the Day of Atonement. You know it begins tonight, the Dia Puro de Senhor, the Pure Day of the Lord. I will pray here with you, here and now.' "

Nobody looked at him as he walked into the back room. Then the old silversmith entered. It took him a while before he came toward Carlebach, but then he looked at the Portuguese prayer book. He tried to read it, but he could not because by now it was too dark for his weak eyes. He asked Carlebach to read it for him.

Carlebach read: "Grande Deus de Israel. Lord of Hosts, accept my fast, my flesh and my bones, as though they were a sacrifice. Look, Father, thou has sent us away, far way, into slavery, without Kohanim, without Levites, without teachers. If we do not do thy will, it is because we don't know any better. If we do not fulfill thy commandments, it is because they torture us and persecute us. Therefore we pray to thee, O Father, save us from torturers and from evil neighbors who betray us. Save us from questions, torture and fire." The old man sat down. Since the words were Portuguese, he had not understood them, but the prayer seemed to have made an impression on him.

He looked at me [Carlebach reports] and his wife came and looked at me fearfully and anxiously. Then he said, "What is that?" I said, "This is a prayer, a Jewish prayer, a prayer for Yom Kippur, Dia Puro."

"Dia Puro," they repeated in a murmur. Then they said, "Dia Puro, today is the day, the day of pardon for all sins, for those who serve in an alien temple."

They began to think. Then something began to dawn on them. It was a dark memory. The inarticulate strange memory of the blood.

Suddenly they asked, *"Hej Yisrael?"* [Because of Israel?]

It was very dark now, the bells from St. Eulalia no longer tolled. The mass had ended. People who had left the church were coming back, stopped at the door of the shop, and they all entered. They gathered around the table in the corner of the room, in front of the kitchen. They were eager to listen and I told them: "There is a town in this world. Its name is Warsaw in a country called Poland. There are a thousand synagogues there. A hundred times a thousand Israelites. Today is Dia Puro, the Pure Day of Forgiveness. The town is empty, the market is dead, the gardens will not be attended. Everybody will have left for the synagogue, for one of the thousand synagogues. There the Jews pray and cry to God, and God listens."

The *chuetas* opened their eyes widely, turned toward me, their faces burning, and now they asked me as though they did not believe me, "A hundred times a thousand Israelites?"

I said, "There is Zion, a fortress on a hill, surrounded by mountains. Jews come from all over, Moscow, Rome, London, and they go up to the mountain and bow down, all of them bow down."

There was silence. The people bowed their heads as though they were in church while Carlebach continued to read the prayer of Yom Kippur: "Grande Deus de Israel. Because we have not thought of the poor and the orphans, evil times have come to us and scattered us to all corners of the world. I pray thee, Grande Deus Adonai, listen to me, according to thy will, but forsake me not, so that the nations may not say, 'Where is your God?,' for I know that God is in heaven. It is He who gives you good and evil."

While he was reading, something was happening. The two old people and the young ones rose, and suddenly there was an echo in the room as the *chuetas* repeated, "Grande Deus de Israel, Adonai." The ice had been broken.

Outside, pots of pork were steaming. Inside, however, it was *Kol Nidre*, the eve of Yom Kippur. According to an old *chueta* custom, candles had been put into a jar; they were lit and they flickered. Then, as Carlebach tells it:

The grandmother of the group rose, and with her, generations of Church Jews and oceans of pain, mountains of persecution and hunt, generations of Jews who lived their lives precariously between the cathedral and the pyres of the auto-da-fé.
These are worlds of lies and suffering. Hearts were tortured
until the last Jewish spark was extinguished. But some little
gleam was left. It was as though somebody had recovered from
a heap of ashes, a glowing atom, which was just about to flicker
a bit, and maybe burn again.

But it did not. It flickered and it was soon extinguished.

After a half-hour, everything was over. Somebody opened the door, light came in, and Carlebach could see once more the indifferent bitterness of their faces. He understood how victorious the Church had been. These were Marranos who would never return to their old faith. Even if they were to enter a synagogue, they would pray to the God of the Holy Trinity. They knew no other God.

The only thing that binds them to us is that until this very
day they suffer because they are known to have been Jews.
They are discriminated against because they are still considered
Jews. This and this alone binds them to us [Carlebach con-
cluded]. As they received me now, as they joined me in speaking of Grande Deus de Israel, the Great God of Israel, as one
of the old women shed tears, and another one embraced me,
it was with the voice of the blood, not of the faith.

They had welcomed Carlebach not as a representative of their people, but only because he did not despise them or hate them. This gave them confidence, even though he was a stranger. The *chuetas* that Carlebach found no longer had any connection with the community of Jews about whom Carlebach had tried to tell them. They did not even really remember the martyrdom of their Jewish ancestors. They were only *chuetas* because the other Majorcans would not let them forget it, because of the strange kind of anti-Semitism which excluded them from the rest of Majorcan society. The only bit of Jewish knowledge that Carlebach's *chuetas* had was the awareness that Grande Deus de Israel had caused them to be martyrs. Whenever they are particularly pressed and in dire need, they say, *"Hej Adonai"*—"because of Adonai." These two words answer many questions: Why must we participate in the holy processions more eagerly than others? Why must at least one member of our family become a priest? Why must our contribution to the church be larger than that of others? Whenever a child asks these questions, the answer is: "Because of Adonai"—*"Hej Adonai."*

But Carlebach was, after all, only a visitor and an outsider among the *chuetas*. What he saw and interpreted as a "shrunken" faith was only the small portion of the *chueta* tradition that a secret sect reluctantly reveals to a complete stranger. Others who have actually lived among the *chuetas* have been able to compile a long list of Jewish customs which exist until this day, and even to collect enough *chueta* prayers to fill a slim volume of liturgy, prepared for their clandestine Jewish services over a period spanning hundreds of years.

For much of our information about these people we are indebted to Baruch Braunstein, who spent many months with the contemporary *chuetas* and studied many of the documents in Spanish archives which deal with the *chuetas* of the Balearic Islands. He also found many of their prayers, some of which are touching documents of a centuries-old devotion to Judaism. Others are expressions of those constant companions of Marranic life, fear, guilt and anxiety, and uniquely express their particular needs. They pray to God to forgive their sins and ask Him to understand their infidelity and have pity on their conflicted twilight existence:

"Our Almighty Father, who daily worketh miracles, take pity on us, O great God, and upon thy innocent flock, who are stung by bees with such great affliction. Thou who art powerful, God eternal, be willing to have pity upon them. Blessed be thy holy name, now and forever. Show us thy light, O Lord, hide it not from us. If our ancestors had sinned for a time, thou, O Lord, didst pardon them; thus saith the Scriptures. Thou, great God, who art in heaven on thy holy throne, have pity on us, great Lord, and upon thy suffering people."

The *chuetas* share a great many customs with the Portuguese Marranos. For instance, when the *chuetas* bake bread they also throw a piece of dough back into the fire. Like so many other Marranic customs, this is considered an old habit. Ask a *chueta* woman why she maintains this strange practice and she will say, "This is the way my mother and my grandmother used to bake bread. It is an old family custom. It adds to the good taste of the bread."

Like the Portuguese Marranos, the *chuetas* of the Balearic Islands refrain from eating meat on the Sabbath to avoid violating the dietary laws. As the family assembles around the table, the father recites the prayer *Recibimiento del Sabat*, the reception of the Sabbath. This prayer is the same

Idus that Schwarz heard in the mountains of Portugal. The Jewish prayer of *Kiddush* is a weekly reminder of the creation of the world and the sanctification of the seventh day. But the Friday-night prayer of the *chuetas* does not even mention the Sabbath. It recalls the story of the blind Tobit who "found the light out of sorrow and blindness." It expresses the Marrano dream, to find their way out of grief and blindness as "Saint Tobit" did. The *chuetas* have a special Sabbath bread and they eat a special Sabbath dish. For the Marranos of Portugal, this dish is fish, but the *chuetas* of Majorca eat a special kind of omelette, not eaten on any other day.

Although by the time Carlebach came to Majorca the *chuetas* hardly remembered Yom Kippur, according to earlier accounts they did observe the holiday during the seventeenth century. They called it "El Ayuno" or "El Dia del Pardon," the Fast or Day of Forgiveness, or "El Ayuno Mayor," the Great Fast. That may be why they didn't understand Carlebach's "Dia Puro de Senhor."

At a trial of the Inquisition in 1677, Pedro Onofre Cortes, who was described as a "descendant of Jews, a native of this city [Palma] of the Calle de Sayel" (the street Carlebach visited), in confessing his "heresy" described the commemoration of the Day of Atonement among the *chuetas* of Palma.

Some *chuetas* remained in the shops to ward off the suspicious guards of the Inquisition. All other members of the community assembled in its large gardens, surrounded by high walls to protect them from curious or dangerous onlookers. The prayers opened strangely with the singing of "Osana, Osana," the Spanish version of the Hebrew word for salvation, the Hosannah of the New Testament which the Jews sing during the festivals of pilgrimage, but never on the Day of Atonement. The men covered their heads with white handkerchiefs which might be a reminder of the tallith, the prayer shawl worn by Jewish men during the morning prayers, or even reminiscent of the white garments which pious Jewish men wear during the whole day of solemn prayers.

It is doubtful that a service conducted in such secrecy could have lasted until sunset. It was probably only a token service at best. Whenever it ended, it is known, it concluded with a ceremony of the "kiss of forgiveness" between members of the congregation.

Because it would have been too difficult to celebrate two major holidays within ten days, the holiday of Rosh Hashanah, the Jewish New Year, was entirely forgotten among the Marranos. But it is remarkable that two and a half centuries following the conversions, Marranos were still celebrating Yom Kippur on the island of Majorca, however strange and distorted their version of the service was.

Among the *chuetas*, fasting is an almost obsessive occupation. The Jewish calendar lists only two major fast days: the Day of Atonement and the ninth day of Av, which commemorates the destruction of the Temple of Jerusalem. The *chuetas* fast much more often even than the very Orthodox Jew, who observes several additional days of fast. The evening meal before the day of fasting is especially elaborate among the *chuetas*. Only new salt is used in the dishes and at the table. Special clothing reserved for fast days is worn. And there is a ceremony of cleansing the body which is meticulously observed.

The *chuetas* also worship Saint Esther, and their Saint Esther Day is a holiday even more sacred than the Day of

Atonement. The Marranos' celebration of the heroism of Esther has little in common with the Jewish holiday of Purim, which celebrates the same happy event, the rescue of the Persian Jewish community from certain destruction. In Jewish tradition, the deliverance from Haman, the arch-enemy, is celebrated in a day of masquerade and merriment. Although the "Scroll of Esther" is read in the synagogue, there is no solemnity attached to it. Each reading of the name of Haman is greeted with a loud noise, and it is certainly the least orderly service of the year. "On Purim," orders a Talmudic admonition, "you must drink so much that in your drunkenness you will no longer remember whether you bless Haman, the evil schemer, or curse Mordecai [Esther's uncle], the Jew who saved the community."

In contrast, among the *chuetas* Saint Esther Day is preceded by three days of fasting. After the fast a ritual bath is taken and new clothing is worn "in memory of the marvels which the God of Israel has done in liberating the children of Israel, and in honor of freedom and triumph over Haman." There is a special holiday menu, reserved for this day and never varied. It consists of fish, spinach and peas. It is a holy meal eaten with sadness and solemnity. "We do it to express our contrition over our apostasy and the betrayal of the faith of our fathers," a *chueta* replied when asked to explain the significance of the holiday.

Passover among the *chuetas* has also completely changed from the traditional Jewish observance, and it differs also from the Pasqua of the Portuguese Marranos. The Seder meal, which is often observed even by Jews who observe no other custom, is unknown. The story of the Exodus from Egypt, which is read from the Haggadah, the book of tales, in traditional Jewish practice, is not even mentioned by the *chuetas*. Their version of the holiday is the feast of the first-born. This is not far removed from Jewish tradition. Passover was always connected with the first-born of Egypt who were slain as part of the ten plagues visited on the Pharaoh, and in whose memory the Orthodox Jewish first-born are supposed to fast on the day preceding Passover. Among the *chuetas*, honoring the first-born constitutes the whole content of the feast. It is in their honor that a whole lamb is roasted and eaten by the family. This, no doubt, is the paschal lamb eaten at the Exodus together with un-leavened bread. But the idea of freedom, the central theme of Passover, is forgotten. Passover, usually a festive and happy holiday, has become a somber reminder of the crypto-Jews' precarious existence and their unrelieved re-morse. "We celebrate it," they say, "because God has cas-tigated us, knowing that we have become idolaters like the Jews of Egypt."

Circumcision has disappeared, for obvious reasons. In the early days on the mainland in Spain, children were still cir-cumcised, and in one of the investigations of the Inquisition it was found that a Judaizing Christian circumcised himself with a piece of glass in jail. But the custom was soon abol-ished. The eighth day in the life of a male child, on which circumcision should take place, is not commemorated at all. Not even a special prayer is said.

But in marriage and death the *chuetas* have preserved some Jewish customs. The marriage ceremonies are, of course, performed by the priest in the local church with all the Catholic rites. But like the other Marranos we have dis-cussed, the *chuetas* marry in two separate ceremonies, once in the church and the other in a form of the "Jewish" wed-ding ritual. The *chueta* version of this Marranic custom is particularly original and colorful. A few days before the day of the marriage they go to the cemetery and visit the graves of their ancestors. There, standing among the crosses which have been placed even on the graves of *chuetas*, the couple recites a prayer called the "Jewish Oath." The community, before consenting to the marriage, has made certain that both bride and groom are descendants of Jewish families.

Intermarriage is strongly discouraged among the *chuetas*. This prohibition is, after all, one of the few ways they have of preserving their fragile heritage. A novel on this theme was written in 1916 by Vicente Blasco-Ibáñez. The book, called *The Dead Command*, describes the difficulties of a marriage between an impoverished Spanish nobleman and the daughter of a rich Marrano from Majorca. In the novel the passionate rejection of intermarriage on the part of the crypto-Jews resulted in this particular marriage never being consummated. And Braunstein tells us that as late as the close of the seventeenth century, the Hebrew word *malshin* (slanderer or denouncer) was applied to anyone who married outside of the Marrano group, and the offspring of such a union were called half-breeds.

Death in the *chueta* community calls for the observance of another set of Jewish customs. When death is approaching, the priest of the Church is called to administer the last rites—unlike the Portuguese custom, which bars the priest. As soon as this is done, the dying *chueta* is turned to face the wall, an old but unexplained Jewish custom. After death, the washing of the body begins in strict observance of the Jewish law which governs this ritual. But first, all the windows are closed—even today—to prevent detection by the spies of the Inquisition. The corpse is washed with water and oil. The body, wrapped in a white shroud, is buried in the Christian cemetery and a cross is placed on the grave. But when the family returns to the privacy of their home, they mourn the dead with Jewish rites. They observe a day of fasting, though this is not a Jewish custom; it has been added by the *chuetas*. After the fast, no food may be cooked in the house of mourning. Neighbors provide the meals, a custom which is observed by Jews all over the world. No meat is eaten during the seven days of mourning lest any dietary laws be violated. And although the Jewish custom of cutting the clothing of the close members of the family has been forgotten by the *chuetas*, they wear the same clothing throughout the thirty days following the funeral service.

Chapter Seven

That the Marranos have survived and that some of them still live their strange separate lives today is in itself amazing. Their clannishness, their secrecy, their ancient guilt, their fear of dangers which threatened their ancestors but which no longer exist, have helped, no doubt, to preserve them. But one of the most remarkable aspects of the Marrano phenomenon is the strange way in which they have transmitted the customs and traditions throughout the generations, and the fact that so many of the same distorted rites, the same variations of old Jewish themes, exist in Marrano communities separated by thousands of miles of land and sea.

How could the Marranos, having burdened themselves with the dual existence in both church and synagogue, transmit any Jewish heritage, however diluted or distorted, from generation to generation? Where did they obtain their information about Jewish customs? How did they preserve these facts for the next generation?

It is usually forgotten that while the Marranos lived in their own peculiar kind of spiritual "captivity," Jewish communities existed in Spain itself until 1492 and were, of course, in existence in other parts of the world. In those early days of the fifteenth and sixteenth centuries, with the memory of the expulsion and the enforced conversions still fresh in their minds, the Jews developed secret signs and even a clandestine language which enabled them to recognize fellow Jews. For although there were many restrictions for Marranos, some were permitted to trade in other countries, as we have seen. One word, one handshake, one twinkle of the eye was often enough for a merchant in Italy to recognize the trader from Spain or Portugal as a fellow Jew.

Of course, the elaborate system of espionage maintained by the Inquisition made them cautious lest they be revealed as "Judaizers," and both the Marrano who had to return to his family back home and the Jew of Venice or Florence with whom he dealt in business understood the imminent dangers their meetings invited. There were family gatherings behind locked doors. Jewish customs were observed as the family sat around the table, and the ceremonial objects which they gave their Marrano visitor as gifts were hidden among the legitimate merchandise he carried back home with him. And often they were disguised. For instance, a menorah, the candelabrum for Hanukkah, might be decorated with a statue of a madonna.

In the fourteenth and fifteenth centuries, some two or three generations after the conversion of their ancestors, the Marranos' most coveted book was a prayer book. In the thorough investigations of the Inquisition, such prayer books were found in the homes of Marranos on the Spanish mainland as well as on the Balearic Islands. Most of them were in Hebrew, although the Marranos by that time no longer understood the language. In the early days of the fourteenth century, some Marranos took Hebrew lessons secretly with priests who themselves were *conversos*. But after a few generations, Hebrew was generally lost to the Marranos, and only a few distorted words—like the *Idus* of the Portuguese or the single word "Adonai"—were left. More important than prayer books in preserving their way of life were Jewish calendars, which were quickly copied and widely distributed. In this way the *chuetas* of Majorca and Ibiza, and the Marranos in other parts of the world, knew when to celebrate the Jewish holidays. Later the dates were only approximately determined, as spring became the time for Passover and autumn for the Day of Atonement.

In fact, since these people had forgotten the meaning of most customs and holidays, and had changed many of the observances and prayers to fit their own needs, after a while almost everything amounted to an approximation. Yet, many Marranic customs in one country resemble those in others. It is understandable that the *chuetas* and the Marranos of the Iberian Peninsula share many of the same rites. But the same customs can also be found in the Caribbean islands and in many South American countries. In their isolation from the rest of Jewry, the rituals they developed became their own authentic Judaism.

For instance, the Marranos have a form of ritual slaughter, a dimly remembered vestige of the Orthodox Jewish direction on killing animals for food. At a meeting of Marranos arranged by Barros Basto in 1926, Rabbi ben Jacob, a Sephardic rabbi of Salonika, had an encounter with a "little clean-shaven man" who told him that he was the *shohet*—the ritual slaughterer—for the community. The rabbi asked him if he really knew the laws concerning ritual slaughter, and if he adhered to them. The man said, "If you don't believe me, why don't you ask the people here." And sure enough, the Marranos replied that the man was, indeed, their *shohet;* they would eat only meat that had been slaughtered by him. There was, however, one small difference between this *shohet* and the *shohet* of Orthodox Jewish communities in other parts of the world. In the first place, he owned no ritual knife, and in the second place, he slaughtered not only cattle but pigs as well. He slaughtered them exactly as the Christian butcher did, but before doing so, he said a Marrano prayer which was addressed to the animal: "Adonai has created you and me. Yet I must kill you. But I want you to know that I have mercy and pity. Praised be Adonai, who gives us food to eat." The *shohet* then explained that he had plans to emigrate to what was at that time Palestine. The rabbi had his doubts that among the Orthodox Jews of Palestine, this particular *shohet* would find ready acceptance.

For although the *shohet*, like all the other Marrano examples we have given, remembered some rudiments of Jewish prayer and custom, there is always a question about the depth of the Jewish identity of the contemporary Marrano. Five hundred years is a long time, but five hundred years without teaching, without any kind of authentic interpretation, without a living, creative community, without history, is eternity. All that is really left is a faint memory, however sacred. Everything from conviction to custom had to be diluted and, of course, much was completely lost. It is miraculous that even the memory, however pale, has survived.

Yet no one can speak of the Marrano who has not returned to his people as being part of Jewish tradition, let alone a member of the Jewish community. The Marranos are a remnant. They have preserved a remnant Judaism in which Esther and even Adonai wear halos. Perhaps that is the reason why Barros Basto's mission ultimately failed. The Marranos he met were not really prepared for Jewish life, and no Jewish school could change that fact. They had lived for so many centuries with subterfuge and in secrecy, and with their special version of Jewish observance, that the transition to open Judaism was too difficult and, perhaps, impossible for them to accomplish.

More recently, there was an attempt to convert to Judaism the *chuetas* of Majorca, but this attempt, like Basto's, and perhaps for the same reasons, also failed. In 1961 a group of Israelis, believing that Jews should have more active missionaries, organized themselves for the purpose of gaining converts to Judaism. In their search for natural objects for conversion, they discovered the *chuetas* of Palma. Israel Lippel, one of the most active members of the group, traveled to Spain, and after spending some time in Barcelona, learning more about the *chuetas*, he went on to Palma.

He met with sixteen heads of families from the *chueta* community and then began to hold meetings in their homes. At these meetings he told *chuetas* about Israel, gave them copies of the Old Testament translated into Spanish, and Spanish-Hebrew dictionaries. He gave each of the women a mezuzah (the tiny scrolls which are attached to the doors of Jewish homes) to wear around her neck, and a larger one to put on the door. He delivered lectures on Zionism and held discussion groups. He had himself photographed with a group of *chuetas*. In the picture he is wearing a prayer shawl, holding a Hebrew book in his hand,

and above him is the crucifix which can be found in every Spanish Catholic home. At the end of his trip he reported that at least three hundred *chuetas* would soon be coming to live in Israel.

A few months later it was reported in the New York *Daily Forward*, a Yiddish-language newspaper, that a letter had been sent from the *chuetas* of Majorca to the Prime Minister of Israel, David Ben-Gurion, asking for permission to enter Israel:

We have heard that God has remembered his people and that after two thousand years the Jewish State has been re-created. We are several thousand men, women and children, the remnants of Spanish Jewry. The cruel Inquisition forced our ancestors to deny their religion and accept the Catholic faith. We appeal to you as the head of the Israeli government to help us to return to the faith of our fathers, to our people and to our homeland. Regretfully we know very little of Jewishness and therefore urge you to supply us with books on Judaism written in the Spanish language. We Marranos yearn to return to our people.

In the end, neither three hundred nor "several thousand" *chueta*s came to Israel. A total of twenty-four men, women and children arrived, and they were admitted as immigrants under the "Law of Return" which guarantees admission to all Jews. But tragically, the *chuetas* thought they could continue to live as they had always lived, under the protection of the Church. They could not cope with the kind of Jewish life they found in Israel. They could establish no relationship with the Israelis, who were foreign to them, not only in language and thought, but also in the customs which they should have had in common. The chief rabbinate of Israel, not known for its liberalism, insisted that the men, regardless of age, immediately undergo circumcision and submit to proper procedures for conversion. The *chuetas*, the rabbis said, had kept no documents through the centuries attesting to the "purity" of their Jewish origins. The whole ill-prepared adventure ended in disaster. The poor *chuetas* who had come with many hopes for a new spiritual experience found that it was not possible in present-day Israel. They quickly returned to Majorca.

If they had stayed, these people would have wanted to take their special kind of worship into the new country with them. Some Marranos have managed to do this. More than a century ago a small group of Marrano immigrants built a little synagogue in Jerusalem. On Yom Kippur, if you passed this small *shul*, you would witness a strange event. At a certain point during the service the congregation would come outside, and in front of the synagogue on the holiest of Jewish holidays, the men would play a game of cards. This was a Marrano habit left over from the days of the Inquisition when in order to fool the guards, they would station men outside their place of secret worship. The card players were set there to divert the officers from the furtive worship that was going on inside. Hundreds of years later this bizarre ceremony was an important part of their worship. It was the only Judaism—the only kind of Yom Kippur service—they had ever known.

In striking contrast, a group of Belgian Marranos successfully immigrated to Israel in 1970. But they were young people, mostly in their thirties, and they had, according to a report in the Jerusalem *Post*, "always fasted on Yom Kippur, eschewed pork, eaten matzo on Passover, and all the males had been circumcised." Members of the community never married in church, only in civil ceremonies. These Marranos were altogether more in touch with authentic Judaism. In fact, their families had hidden from the Nazis during the war for fear of being identified as Jews. "We felt different and people knew we were," one of their members said.

They had emigrated from Italy in a group and settled in Liège, where they lived in a large community of people who considered themselves Marranos, but they had gradually made up their minds to return to Judaism. Several Jews had helped them get jobs in Liège. After a time they appealed to the Belgian rabbinate for conversion and for assistance in immigrating to Israel. Because of their Italian background the chief rabbi of Rome was called in, and after a year's inquiry he ruled that eleven families were really of Marrano origin and could convert. Between Rosh Hashanah and Yom Kippur of 1970 they went to Italy and were officially converted: the women took ritual baths, the men were subjected to a special ritual which made their circumcisions official, and the children were given Jewish names. Then they immigrated to Israel.

Unlike the *chuetas*, the Marranos of Liège knew exactly what to expect when they got to Israel. "We decided to come for the sake of our children's future," said one of them, a young man wearing a skull cap. "We know that this is the only country where we can live as real Jews, and openly so. This is what we want."

The Marrano is clearly defined by the historic terms of time and place. The Christian Marrano or *chueta* is the product of historic processes in Spain and Portugal of the fourteenth and fifteenth centuries. The Mohammedan Marrano is the product of the conversion of Shabtai Zvi in the seventeenth century.

While he lives as an uneasy convert, the Marrano's

Judaism is an illicit, underground faith, the religion of the secret Jew, the Jew in hiding who practices a few, often misunderstood Jewish customs clandestinely. An open, recognized Judaism is beyond the Marrano's experience. To him, Judaism is the skeleton in his closet. He is not necessarily ashamed of it, but he is frightened by its consequences. Long after the Inquisition was dead, the fear of discovery was very much alive.

To many scholars, Marranism is only a peculiar aspect of Jewish history. To me, it is an important factor in what one might call the "Jewish condition." How else explain those modern Jews who know that their ancestors were Marranos but who have no other links with either Judaism or the Jewish people? The reasons they have not forgotten may be a psychiatric or even a mystical problem, beyond ordinary logic. There are today, throughout the world, but particularly in Spain, Portugal and Latin America, many such people. Their "historic memory" no longer constitutes a personal burden. On the contrary, it is often—as in the case of many present-day Spanish intellectuals—a source of great pride and a proof of their ancestral uniqueness. Whatever it is, it exists.

One of the most dramatic stories of this mysterious Marranic existence was told to me by the late Moshe Sharett, former Secretary of Foreign Affairs and Prime Minister of Israel. It took place in the autumn of 1947, when the Zionists were anxiously awaiting the great United Nations debate which would create a Jewish state or destroy hope for it. During the months before that historic meeting, Zionist leaders engaged in feverish activity to win the votes of the member states of the United Nations. Every bit of information was carefully scrutinized, and if there was any doubt of a positive vote, contacts were established to convince the wavering government of the justice of the Jewish cause.

Dr. Chaim Weizmann, later President of Israel, was told that a certain South American government had decided to vote against the creation of the Jewish state in deference to its large and influential Arab population. Moshe Sharett and Weizmann carefully planned a visit to the ambassador of that Latin American country, and a full history of the man they were to see was assembled.

Weizmann and Sharett were cordially welcomed by the diplomat. Weizmann presented the case of the Jewish people, bereft of six million, one third of its population, desperately in need of a country which they could call their own.

The diplomat seemed ill at ease. When Weizmann paused, he said, "Gentlemen, my government and I are painfully aware of the great suffering of your people, but . . ."

At this moment Weizmann rose suddenly, looked straight into the eyes of the diplomat and said with a trembling voice, "Your Excellency, may I say to you at this private meeting that is not becoming for you to speak of the Jews as '*your* people.' I know enough about you and your family to say that you ought to be speaking about '*my* people.' The blood of the Jews which runs in my veins flows in yours as well. You are the descendant of a Marrano family."

The diplomat paled and his hands shook when he escorted his guests to the door. His government did not vote against the Jewish state.

The Marranos adventure continues today. New Marranos have been discovered in Mexico. Seven thousand of them who live in the Peralvillo district of Mexico City have returned to Judaism, which they call the "Church of God." These mestizos, who have retained Jewish customs and "remember" their Jewish ancestors who came to Mexico with the Spaniards, now have a synagogue of their own and treasure their Torah scrolls, which they received from American Jews. Other Marranos live, though often secretly, in Venta Prieta, Toluca, Cocula and Apipilco.

In Monterrey, in the Mexican state of Nuevo León, where a number of mestizos now openly confess their Jewish origin, the Catholic church of the Christian *indios* is still called El Synagoga. The religious and psychological problems of these *indios* have not as yet been examined. But there is no reason to believe that their concepts of Judaism as a secret cult, their ignorance of Jewish history or the meaning of Jewish tradition will be very different from the *chuetas* of Majorca or the Marranos of Portugal.

These cases of actual and genuine Marranos are simple enough. But Marranism as a "Jewish condition" is of a completely different character. It is a phenomenon of the modern Jew. More than a hundred thousand Jews converted to Christianity between the time of the French Revolution and the beginning of the twentieth century. Many more continued their lives, unconverted, but totally separated from the Jewish people or its faith. They are known as "assimilated Jews." (The assimilated Jew is not to be confused with what we may call the "acculturated Jew"—who is a member of the society of the country in which he lives, who shares its language, its mores, its aspirations, but preserves his allegiance to the Jewish people, its traditions, its hopes and its anxieties. He is not always a religious Jew maintaining customs and beliefs of the Jewish faith, yet his "Jewishness" is undenied and he has no desire to change it.)

The assimilated Jew of whom we speak is one of "Jewish descent," who may deny it, hide it or be ashamed of it. Like the Marrano, his Jewishness is the skeleton in his closet. He would prefer to associate with "others" rather than cultivate his Jewishness. In many respects he is very much a modern Marrano. For although he is trying to keep his Jewish origin secret, he remains latently Jewish. There was a time when this type of Jew was a rarity. We are approaching the time when he may represent a majority of the Jewish community. Religious and secular ties are becoming less binding. A very large number of young Jewish people throughout the world have only tenuous ties with their Jewishness. But—and this is the problem which reminds us so much of the Marranos—*can Jewishness be forgotten?*

As the fate of the Jew is unique, illogical, alarming and vexing, so is the very fact of the existence of an ancient people in the modern world a great riddle. Theologians weigh the question of a divinely ordained continuity of Jewish history. Christian theology has sometimes claimed that the very existence of the Jews was God's punishment for collective sins. Like Cain, we wander from country to country into the arms of merciless persecution which, according to these theologians, we richly deserve.

But such persecutions are no longer in vogue. The Jews exist even in a more peaceful world. Is there an unseen, an invisible hand that guides the destinies of the only ancient people still around? Are we to be the living witnesses of Hebrew antiquity, the great and the tragic experiences of Egypt, Babylon and Palestine? So some people believe. Yet all these are speculations with little expectation of sound and sane analysis. There is only one clear fact: Jews are.

Yet, as religious values evaporate, as the number of intermarriages grows, as we come closer to Jewish integration into the general community, we have to face what Jews will be like fifty or a hundred years hence: many synagogues will no doubt have closed. Much of the battle for Jewish identity and the creative continuity of Jewish civilization will have been lost, and then we will be faced with the real problem of the new Marranos. Though a small, deeply committed Jewish community will continue to exist, the "Marrano community" will be larger. A few customs may be remembered. Some memories, anecdotes, jokes, little sentimentalities—but probably not much more.

Yet, Marranism is also the story of Jewish tenacity, the Jew's incredible talent for survival. As the Marranos of the fifteenth century, in a very deep sense, helped the Jewish people to survive in spite of indescribable cruelties, so will there be left in the Marranos of the year 2030 some residue of "Jewishness," which may, perhaps, be enough to preserve for the Jewish spirit the glorious reputation of invincibility.

Source References

PAGE

8. "The Jews of the Sahara Desert . . ." Nahum Slouschz, *Travels in North Africa.*

20. "These Jews, who were for the most part rich . . ." Valeriu Marcu, *The Expulsion of the Jews from Spain.*

21. "The impetus of those who directed . . ." Quoted, *ibid.*

22. "Jews are a people . . . any medicine or cathartic made by a Jew. . . ." These portions are taken from the Seven Part Code quoted in Jacob R. Marcus, *The Jew in the Medieval World.*

28. "If I were to tell you here . . ." Rabbi Crescas letter quoted in Yitzchak Baer, *A History of the Jews in Christian Spain.*

30. "They came forward demanding baptism . . ." Henry Kamen, *The Spanish Inquisition.*

32. Heinrich Heine, *Hebräische Melodien.*

33. "They simply assimilate . . ." From the prayer *Alenu:* "Make us not like the other nations of the world."

38. "At the end of the fifteenth century . . ." Kamen, *op. cit.*

40. "These heretics avoid baptizing . . ." Quoted in Baer, *op. cit.,* Vol. I.

PAGE

41. "Raise your eyes and see. . . ." Solomon Ibn Verga, *The Tribe of Judah.*

45. "Changing the body linen . . . the justice of the result." Henry C. Lea, *Inquisition of Spain.*

54. "Trusting in the vain hopes . . ." Quoted in Madariaga, *Christopher Columbus.*

56. "eccentric traveller . . ." *Ibid.*

56. He "looked and sounded . . ." *Ibid.*

56. "After the Spanish monarchs had expelled . . ." *Ibid.*

56. "at the great auto-da-fé at Tarragona . . ." *Ibid.*

60. Re "purity of blood." Kamen, *op. cit.*

63. "A Spanish cleric . . ." Lea, *op. cit.*

65. "Memorial for the Coming Generations." Carl Gebhart, ed., *Die Schriften des Uriel da Costa* (author's trans.).

65. Rabbi Uri Halevi's account, *ibid.*

73. . . . these Marranos "who have left the idolatry . . ." *Ibid.*

74. "There is another group that returns . . ." *Ibid.*

76. "I was born in Portugal . . ." and all quotes in this chapter by Uriel da Costa, *ibid.*

87. "The leaders of the Jewish community . . . published or written by him." Quoted in Jacob Freudenthal, *Die Lebensgeschichte Spinozas* (author's trans.).

89. Spinoza was of "medium size . . ." Johannes Colerus, *Levensbeschryving van Benedictus de Spinoza* (author's trans.).

90. "Spinoza learned daily . . ." Jacob Freudenthal, *Spinoza, Leben und Lehre* (author's trans.).

97. "When, in 1672, French armies . . ." *Ibid.*

102. "*Esperanza* is the Jewish characteristic . . ." Yosef Hayim Yerushalmi, *From Spanish Court to Italian Ghetto.*

102. "When the Messiah comes to Spain . . ." *Ibid.*

102. Abraham Cardoso quote, *ibid.*
seh ben Israel.

107. Fernandez Caravajal quote, in Cecil Roth, *A Life of Menas-*

PAGE

107. Burton quote, *ibid.*

108. "These are the boons and the favor . . ." Quoted in Marcus, *op. cit.*

109. Cromwell's edict, *ibid.*

109. "Religious toleration challenged all the beliefs . . ." Winston S. Churchill, *A History of the English-Speaking Peoples,* Vol. II.

115. "Some sold all their worldly goods . . ." M. Lowenthal (trans.), *Memoirs of Glueckel or Hameln.*

119. The ten commandments of the *doenmebs.* Gershom Scholem, *Doenmeb's Prayer Service.*

126. "A contemporary source . . ." Quoted in Baer, *op. cit.*

127. "Among the free inhabitants . . ." Werner Sombart, *Die Juden und das Wirtschaftsleben* (author's trans.).

128. Governor of Jamaica, quoted *ibid.*

129. King Henry II's proclamation; a report to Charles V; instructions for Bordeaux. *Ibid.*

131. Quotes re Joseph Nasi, in Cecil Roth, *The House of Nasi.*

134. Royal decree of 1537, in Marcus, *op. cit.*

135. Message to Thomas Cromwell, in Roth, *The House of Nasi.*

136. "The accused is not quite guilty . . ." *Ibid.*

138. "not in the neighborhood . . ." Marcus, *op. cit.*

139. "had impoverished Spain . . ." Roth, *op. cit.*

140. "betrayed his faith . . ." S. M. Dubnow, *Weltgeschichte des jüdischen Volkes* (author's trans.).

145. Suleiman's letter to the pope, quoted in Roth, *op. cit.*

147. "It is your destiny . . ." *Ibid.*

147. The story of Rabbi Joseph ben Ardut, from Joseph HaKohen's *The Vale of Tears,* quoted in Marcus, *op. cit.*

156. The customs of the Jews in Beira Baixa and Monsanto, in Samuel Schwarz, *Os Cristãos-Novos em Portugal no seculo XX* (author's trans.).

157. "This is the case of Juan Méndez . . ." Quoted in Lucien Wolf, *Jews in the Canary Islands.*

PAGE

158. "I arrived in Braganza ..." Quoted in Cecil Roth, *L'Apô tre des marranes* (author's trans.).

159. Prayer of Marrano women in Braganza, quoted in Schwarz, *op. cit.*

161. Schwarz's experiences in Belmonte, *ibid.*

168. The material regarding the Marranos in Palma de Majorca is based on Ezriel Carlebach, *Exotische Juden* (author's trans.).

Bibliography

Abrahams, Israel, *Jewish Life in the Middle Ages*, Cecil Roth, ed. London, 1932.

Adler, Elkan Nathan, *Auto De Fé and Jew*. London, 1908.

——, *Documents sur les Marranes d'Espagne et de Portugal sous Phillippe IV* (Révue des Études juives). Paris, 1904.

Altmann, Alexander, ed., *Jewish Medieval and Renaissance Studies*. Cambridge, Mass., 1967.

Azevedo, I. L., *Historia dos Christãos Novos Portuguese*. Lisbon, 1921.

Baer, Yitzchak, *A History of the Jews in Christian Spain*. 2 vols. Philadelphia, 1966.

Baron, Salo W., *A Social and Religious History of the Jews*, Vol. 11, New York–Philadelphia, 1967.

Beinart, Haim, *The Records of the Inquisition* (in Hebrew). Tel Aviv, 1965.

Blasco-Ibáñez, Vicente, *The Dead Command*. New York, 1919.

Bloom, Herbert Ivan, *Economic Activities of the Marrannes Jews in Holland in the 17th Century*. Williamsport, Pa., 1937.

Braunstein, Baruch, "Jews in Many Lands—The Island of Majorca." *B'Nai B'Rith Magazine* (March 1934).

Braunstein, Baruch, *The Chuetas of Majorca*. Columbia Univ. Oriental Series, Vol. XXVIII. Scranton, Pa., 1936.

Cambridge Modern History, A. W. Ward, Sir G. W. Prothero and Sir Stanley Leathes, eds. Vol. I. London, 1934.

Carlebach, Ezriel, *Exotische Juden*. Berlin, 1932.

Caro, Georg, *Sozial und Wirtschaftsgeschichte der Juden im Mittelalter und der Neuzeit*. Frankfurt, 1908.

Castro, A., *Spanien, Vision und Wirklichkeit*. Berlin, 1957.

Cervantes, *Don Quixote*. Baltimore, 1967.

Churchill, Winston, S., *A History of the English-Speaking Peoples*, Vol. II, *The New World, 1485–1688*. New York, 1956.

Colerus, Johannes, *Levensbeschryving van Benedictus de Spinoza*. 1705.

Coulton, G. G., *The Inquisition*. New York, 1929.

"Crypto-Jews of Portugal, The," *Menorah Journal*, Vol. XII (1926).

Danon, Abraham, *A Jewish Moslem Sect in Turkey*. Sokolov Year Book, 1900.

David, M., *Who Was Columbus?* New York, 1933.

Dubnow, S. M., *History of the Jews in Russia and Poland*, Vol. 1. Philadelphia, 1916.

———, *Weltgeschichte des jüdischen Volkes*. Berlin, 1928.

Ehrenpreis, Marc, *Le Pays entre Orient et Occident*. Paris, 1927.

Eliacheff, Boris, "Chez les Chrétiens marranes de Medellin," *Le Monde* (August 27, 1968).

Emanuel, Charles H. L., *A Century and a Half of Jewish History*. London, 1910.

Epstein, Isidore, *The Responsa of Rabbi Simon B. Zemah Duran As a Source of the History of the Jews in North Africa*. London, 1930.

Evans, Austin P., "Social Aspects of Medieval Heresy," in *Persecution and Liberty*. New York, 1931.

Extracts from Trial 4427 of Henriques Brites (by the Inquisition of Lisbon, 1675).

Farinelli, Arturo, *Marrano*. Geneva, 1925.

Fast, Howard, *Torquemada*. Garden City, N.Y., 1966.

Fergusson, D., *Trial of Gabriel de Granada by the Inquisition in Mexico, 1642–1645*, Vol. VII. London, 1899.

Finkelstein, Louis, *Jewish Self-Government in the Middle Ages*. Philadelphia, 1924.

Fischel, W., *Marrano Community in Persia*. Jerusalem, 1935.

Freudenthal, Jacob, *Spinoza, Leben und Lehre*. Heidelberg, 1927.

———, *Die Lebensgeschichte Spinozas*. Leipzig, 1899.

Gebhardt, Carl, *Spinoza, Vier Reden*. Heidelberg, 1928.

Gebhardt, Carl, ed., *Die Schriften des Uriel da Costa*. Heidelberg, 1922.

———, *Leone Ebreo, Dialoghi d'amore, Hebräische Gedichte*. Heidelberg, 1929.

Ginsburger, M., *Des Marranes à Colmar*. Paris, 1933.

———, *Marie de Hongrie, Charles Quint, les Veuves Mendes et les Neo-Chrétiens*. Paris, 1934.

Graetz, H., *La Police de l'Inquisition d'Espagne à sa débuts*. Paris, 1893.

Ha-Lapid magazine (1927–33). Lisbon.

Heine, Heinrich, *Hebräische Melodien*. Munich, 1929.

Hume, Martin A. S., *Spain, Its Greatness and Decay (1479–1788)*. Cambridge Historical Series. Cambridge, 1940.

Hyamson, A. M., *The Sephardim of England*. London, 1951.

Ibn Verga, Solomon, *The Tribe of Judah*. (Fifteenth-century Spain, often quoted.)

Isaacs, A. Lionel, *The Jews of Majorca*. London, 1936.

Jacobs, Joseph, *An Inquiry into the Sources of the History of the Jews in Spain*. London, 1894.

Jost, J. M., *Geschichte des Judenthums und seiner Sekten*. Leipzig, 1857–59.

Kamen, Henry, *The Spanish Inquisition.* New York, 1965.

Kastein, Joseph, *Shabtai Zevi, Messiah of Ismir.* Berlin, 1921.

————, *Uriel da Costa.* Berlin, 1932.

Kayserling, M., *Geschichte der Juden in Portugal.* Berlin, 1867.

————, *Die Juden in Navarra, den Baskenländern und auf den Balearen.* Berlin, 1861.

————, *Zur Geschichte der Juden in Barcelona.* Berlin, 1867.

————, *Auto de fé and Jews.* New York, 1901.

————, *Biblioteca Española-Portugueza-Judaica.* Strassburg, 1890.

————, *Die Juden auf Mallorca.* Jahrbuch für die Geschichte der Juden und des Judenthums, Vol. I. Berlin, 1860.

Keller, Werner, *Diaspora.* New York, 1960.

Kelly, Eleanor, *Sea Change.* New York, 1931.

Kober, Adolf, *Jewish Converts in Provence from the 16th to the 18th Century.* New York, 1944.

Kober, Franz, ed., *A Treasury of Jewish Letters.* New York, 1952.

Lea, Henry C., *Inquisition of Spain.* 4 vols. New York, 1906.

Lerner, Ira T., *Mexican Jewry in the Land of the Aztecs.* Mexico City, 1967.

Levy, M. A., *Die Sephardim in Bosnien.* Sarajevo, 1911.

Lewis, A., "Die Neuchristen auf der Insel Mallorca," *Jüdisches Literaturblatt*, XII (Magdeburg, 1883).

Lindo, Elias Hiam, *The History of the Jews in Spain and Portugal.* New York, 1970.

Lloyd, Alan, *The Spanish Centuries.* Garden City, N.Y., 1968.

Loeb, O., *La Correspondance des juifs d'Espagne avec eux de Constantinople.* Paris, 1936.

————, *Le Nombre des juifs de Castille et d'Espagne.* Parıs, 1887.

Lowenthal, M., *Memoirs of Glueckel of Hameln* (translated), Philadelphia, 1932.

Madariaga, Salvador de, *Spain.* New York, 1931.

Madariaga, Salvador de, *Christopher Columbus*. New York, 1940.

Marcu, Valeriu, *The Expulsion of the Jews from Spain*. New York, 1935.

Marcus, Jacob R., *The Jew in the Medieval World*. Cincinnati, 1938.

——, *Notes on Sephardic Jewish History of the 16th Century*, Vol. I, Cincinnati, 1925.

Morel, Fatio A., *Notes et documents pour servir à l'histoire des juifs des Baleares sous les dominations aragoniennes du XIIIᵉ au XVᵉ siècles*. Paris, 1938.

Netanyanu, Ben-Zion, *The Marranos of Spain*. Philadelphia, 1966.

Neuman, Abraham A., *The Jews in Spain*, Vols. I and II. Philadelphia, 1942.

Pflaum, H., *Une ancienne satire espagnole contre les marranes*. Paris, 1928.

Poliakov, Leon, *Histoire de l'antisémitisme, de Mahomet aux marranes*. Paris, 1961.

Pons, A., *Los judéos del reino de Mallorca, Hispania XVI*. Madrid, 1958.

Porges, N., *Zur Lebensgeschichte Uriel da Costas*. Leipzig, 1918.

Portuguese Marranos Committee. Bevis Marks Synagogue. London, 1938.

Prins, Izak, *De Vestiging der Marranen in Noord Nederland in de zestiende Eeuw*. Amsterdam, 1927.

Revah, I. S., *Les Marranes*. Paris, 1959.

——, *Autobiographie d'un marrane*. Paris, 1961.

Reznik, J., *Le Duc De Naxos*. Paris, 1936.

Rivkin, Ellis, *The Shaping of Jewish History*. New York, 1971.

Rodriguez-Monino, A., *Les Judaisants à Badajos de 1493 à 1599*. 1955.

Roth, Cecil, *Neue Kunde von der Marranen Gemeinde in Hamburg*. Berlin, 1930.

Roth, Cecil, *A History of the Marranos*. Philadelphia, 1966.

———, *Notes sur les marranes de Livourne*. Paris, 1931.

———, *Les Marranes à Venice*. Paris, 1930.

———, *Les Marranes à Rouen*. Paris, 1932.

———, *L'Apôtre des marranes*. Paris, 1930.

———, *Jews, Conversos, and the Blood Accusation in 15th Century Spain*. London, 1932.

———, *Immanuel Aboab's Proselytization of the Marranos*. London, 1932.

———, *The Ritual Murder Libel and the Jew*. London, 1934.

———, *A Life of Menasseh ben Israel*. Philadelphia, 1934.

———, *The Spanish Inquisition*. London, 1937.

———, *Marranos and Racial Antisemitism*. Jewish Social Studies. London, 1940.

———, *The House of Nasi*. Philadelphia, 1947.

Scholem, Gershom, *Die krypto-jüdische sekte der Doenmeh in der Türkei*. Leiden, 1931.

———, *Doenmeh's Prayer Service*. New York, 1942.

———, *Sprouting of the Horn of the Son of David* (In the time of Herod). New York, 1963.

———, *Der Messianismus der Sabbatianer*. Frankfurt, 1963.

———, *The Messianic Idea in Judaism*. New York, 1971.

Schwarz, Samuel, *Os Cristãos-Novos em Portugal no seculo XX*. Lisbon, 1925.

Sicroff, Albert A., *Les Controverses des statuts de "pureté de sang" en Espagne du XVe au XVIIe siècles*. Paris, 1960.

Silver, Abba Hillel, *A History of the Messianic Speculation in Israel*. New York, 1927.

Slouschz, Nahum, *Travels in North Africa*. Philadelphia, 1927.

Sombart, Werner, *Die Juden und das Wirtschaftsleben*. Munich, 1928.

Sonne, O., *Da Costa Studies*, Vol. XXII. New York, 1931.

Szajkowski, Zosa, *Notes on the Languages of the Marranos and Sephardim in France*. New York, 1964.

Wolf, Lucien, *Jews in the Canary Islands.* London, 1925.

―――, *The Marranos in Portugal.* London, 1925.

―――, *Menassah ben Israel's Mission to Oliver Cromwell.* London, 1901.

Yerushalmi, Yosef Hayim, *From Spanish Court to Italian Ghetto: Isaac Cardoso, A Study in 17th Century Marranism and Jewish Apologetics.* New York and London, 1971.

Zunz, Leopold, *Gesammelte Schriften,* Vol. II, *1875–1876.* Berlin.

About the Author

JOACHIM PRINZ served as president of the American Jewish Congress from 1958 to 1966, when he retired and was elected honorary president. He was one of the ten founding chairmen of the 1963 March on Washington. Born in Germany, Dr. Prinz was a rabbi in the Jewish community of Berlin and was one of the first Jewish leaders in Germany to speak out against Nazism and to urge the immediate mass migration of Jews from Europe to Palestine. He was expelled from Germany in 1937 and came to the United States. He is the author of *Dilemma of the Modern Jew* and *Popes from the Ghetto* as well as numerous other books in both German and English. He lectures extensively and lives with his family in New Jersey, where he is rabbi of a large congregation.